REPORT ON EXAMINATION

OF

GERMAN A.F.V.

8-WHEEL DRIVE, 8-WHEEL STEERING

REPORT ON EXAMINATION

OF

GERMAN A.F.V.

8-WHEEL DRIVE, 8-WHEEL STEERING

> We desire to acknowledge the valuable assistance we have received from the Director of Tank Design and the following firms:
>
> Messrs. Bendix Ltd.
> Messrs. C. A. V. Ltd.
> Messrs. W. T. Flather Ltd.
> The Hoffmann Manufacturing Co. Ltd.
> Messrs. Solex Ltd.
>
> *Engineering Department,*
> *DENNIS BROS., LTD.,*
> *Guildford*

The Naval & Military Press Ltd

Published by

The Naval & Military Press Ltd
Unit 5 Riverside, Brambleside
Bellbrook Industrial Estate
Uckfield, East Sussex
TN22 1QQ England

Tel: +44 (0)1825 749494

www.naval-military-press.com
www.nmarchive.com

In reprinting in facsimile from the original, any imperfections are inevitably reproduced and the quality may fall short of modern type and cartographic standards.

CONTENTS

	PAGE
INTRODUCTION	4
GENERAL DESCRIPTION OF COMPLETE VEHICLE	5
GENERAL DATA OF COMPLETE VEHICLE	6
FRAME	9
ENGINE	10
CLUTCH	23
COUPLING SHAFTS	23
GEARBOX	24
FINAL DRIVE	28
HUBS AND STUB AXLES	32
WHEELS AND TYRES	33
SUSPENSION	34
STEERING GEAR	37
BRAKING SYSTEM	40
RADIATOR	41
FUEL SYSTEM	43
CHASSIS LUBRICATION	43
ELECTRICAL EQUIPMENT	43
HULL	44
TURRET	45
PERFORMANCE	48
ANALYSIS OF PERFORMANCE (APPENDIX A)	51
ANALYSIS OF COMPONENTS (APPENDIX B)	52

LIST OF ILLUSTRATIONS

Fig. No.	Subject	Page
1	COMPLETE VEHICLE, ¾ REAR	4
2	,, ,, ¾ FRONT	5
3	,, ,, FRONT END	5
4	CHASSIS, ¾ FRONT	6
5	,, SIDE ELEVATION	7
6	,, REAR ,,	8
7	,, ¾ REAR	9
8	ENGINE, CROSS-SECTION	11
9	,, LONG ,,	11
10	,, CYLINDER BLOCK	12
11	,, ,, ,, INVERTED	12
12	,, ,, LINERS	12
13	,, ,, HEAD	13
14	,, PISTONS AND CONNECTING RODS	13
15	,, CRANKSHAFT, ¾ END VIEW	14
16	,, ,, BROADSIDE	14
17	,, TIMING GEAR	15
18	,, ,, ,, SECTION	16
19	,, VALVE OPERATION	16
20	,, OIL DIAGRAM	19
21	,, OIL BY-PASS	19
22	,, AUXILIARY-DRIVE SECTION	20
23	,, COMPLETE, FLYWHEEL-END	20
24	,, ,, TIMING END	21
25	GEARBOX, CONTROL DIAGRAM	24
26	,, CASING ASSEMBLED	24
27	,, LONGITUDINAL SECTION	25
28	,, CROSS SECTION AB	25
29	,, ,, ,, CD	25
30	,, SELECTOR MECHANISM	26
31	,, CASING EXPLODED	27
32	TRANSMISSION, DIAGRAM OF LAY-OUT	28
33	,, FINAL-DRIVE COMPLETE	28
34	,, FREE-WHEEL COMPONENTS	29
35	,, DIFFERENTIAL COMPONENTS	30
36	,, FREE-WHEEL DIAGRAM	30
37	TRANSMISSION, LONGITUDINAL SECTION	31
38	,, CROSS SECTION	31
39	,, HUB BEARINGS	32
40	SUSPENSION, LONG ELEVATION	34
41	,, SECTION THROUGH CHASSIS CROSS-MEMBER	34
42	,, SECTION THROUGH PIVOTS	35
43	,, ELEVATION OF SPRING	35
44	,, LINKS AND BRACKET	35
45	,, DIAGRAM OF ARTICULATION	36
46	,, LOAD-DIAGRAM OF ARTICULATION	36
47	STEERING, ORTHOGRAPHIC VIEW	37
48	,, LINKAGE DIAGRAM	37
49	,, TRACK LINKS	38
50	,, COUPLING GEAR	39
51	BRAKE, ELEVATION AND SECTION	40
52	RADIATOR, FAN SIDE	41
53	,, OIL-COOLER SIDE	42
54	HULL AND TURRET, PLAN AND ELEVATION	44
55	,, ,, ,, REAR VIEW	44
56	,, ,, ,, FRONT VIEW	44
57	,, INTERIOR VIEW	45
58	TURRET CONTROLS, DIAGRAM OF ARRANGEMENT	45
59	,, ,, COMMANDER'S TRAVERSING GEAR	46
60	,, ,, GUNNER'S TRAVERSING GEAR	46
61	,, ,, GUNNER'S ELEVATING GEAR, CROSS SECTION	46
62	,, ,, GUNNER'S ELEVATING GEAR, LONGITUDINAL SECTION	47
63	,, ,, SHOWING CLUTCH DRUMS	47
64	PERFORMANCE DIAGRAM, CORNERING	49
65	,, ,, TRENCH CROSSING	50

LIST OF TABLES

Table No.	Subject	Page
1	GEAR RATIOS AND SPEEDS	6
2	FRAME DIMENSIONS	9
3	ENGINE DIFFERENCES	10
4	CYLINDER-BLOCK DIMENSIONS	12
5	CYLINDER-HEAD DIMENSIONS	12
6	PISTON DIMENSIONS AND WEIGHTS	13
7	CONNECTING-ROD DIMENSIONS AND WEIGHTS	13
8	CRANKSHAFT DIMENSIONS	15
9	CAMSHAFT ,,	16
10	VALVE-GEAR ,, AND WEIGHTS	17
11	CAM CHARACTERISTICS	18
12	OIL-PUMP DIMENSIONS	18
13	WATER ,, ,,	20
14	INDUCTION DIMENSIONS	22
15	COUPLING ,,	23
16	GEARBOX GEAR DATA	27
17	FINAL-DRIVE, TOOTH-LOADING	29
18	HUB AND STUB-AXLE LOADING	32
19	SUSPENSION SYSTEM, WEIGHTS	35
20	UNSPRUNG WEIGHTS	35
21	LOADING OF RUBBER BEARINGS	36
22	LEAF-SPRING DATA	36
23	WHEEL CAMBER	38
24	DATA OF TURRET-CONTROL CLUTCHES	48
25	DATA OF TURRET GEARS	48
26	ANGLES OF ROLL	49

INTRODUCTION

In July, 1942, two German 8-wheeled armoured cars which had been captured in the Middle East were delivered to Dennis Bros., Ltd., who were instructed to attempt the repair of one vehicle and to make a report giving constructional particulars.

Both the vehicles had been disabled by shell-fire. In addition, many parts were missing and the general condition of the vehicles was poor, due to neglect and damage received in transit.

One of the vehicles, referred to as an Armoured Fighting Vehicle (A.F.V.), was fitted with a turret; A.C.V. into running order by stripping out all damaged units and substituting sound units taken from the A.F.V. chassis.

Units treated in this way included the front final drive and suspension assembly, and certain propellor shafts, wheel-hub assemblies and tyres.

The engine, No. 67815, was completely stripped and overhauled. Other units were checked for defects, as far as possible, without stripping.

After the chassis of the A.C.V. had been repaired and painted, it was fitted with the hull of the A.F.V.,

Fig. 1. A semi-plan, ¾ rear view of the composite vehicle resulting from the work carried out by Dennis Bros. Ltd. (A.C.V. chassis with A.F.V. hull).

the other (A.C.V.), being designed as an Armoured Command Vehicle, had no turret.

Other major differences between the two vehicles were found to be as under:—

	A.F.V.	A.C.V.
Engine number	67186	67815
Engine Block material	Cast-iron	Aluminium Alloy
Clutch, make	Fichtel & Sachs	Long

Apart from the above differences, all units were practically interchangeable.

The engine block of the A.F.V. had been pierced from end to end by a shell, but the engine of the A.C.V. appeared repairable.

It was therefore decided to put the chassis of the the mounting holes having to be elongated for this purpose.

Performance trials, the results of which appear later in this report, were then carried out by the Experimental Wing, D.T.D.

Owing to the importance attached to reconditioning the A.C.V. chassis as quickly as possible, time was not available to obtain complete technical data of this chassis, and the dimensions, etc., given in the report are therefore based on examination of the units of the A.F.V. chassis.

The remarks in the report dealing with the condition of parts as stripped refer to the engine of the A.C.V. and in respect of other units, to those of the A.F.V. The speedometer reading of the A.F.V. when captured was 8,463 kilometres.

GENERAL DESCRIPTION

This class of vehicle, which has drive and steering on all eight wheels, is provided with controls duplicated at each end, to enable it to be driven in either direction at full speed. All units, except the radiator, appear to have been designed to function equally well in either direction of running.

Considerable care has been taken, in the general design, to hold weight to a minimum, and comparatively thin armour has been adopted; a relatively high power-weight ratio and good performance have been achieved as a partial consequence.

A single eight-cylinder V-type petrol engine, mounted at the normal rear end of the vehicle, drives forward to a central gearbox which gives six speeds in either direction, and is controlled by two levers and a reversing pedal.

The suspension may be described as independent, in that upward movement of a wheel does not necessarily involve movement of the opposite wheel. There is, however, provision for equalising the loading of the longitudinally adjacent wheels of a bogie. Rubber bearings of the Silentbloc type have been largely used in the suspension, in which a high ratio of sprung to unsprung weight has been obtained.

The steering system is complex but geometrically orthodox, except that certain details, considered in conjunction with the operation of the suspension, tend to introduce instability in steering control.

There are two unusual features in the final drive; one is the cam-type differential between the axle shafts, and the other is the provision of the freewheels between the outer and intermediate axles, to permit the front and rear axles to over-run the others, a condition that becomes necessary on lock.

No booster is provided for the wedge-expanded, self-energising brakes which are applied through the medium of cables.

An elaborate system of chassis lubrication enables numerous points to be pressure-fed with oil from the engine at the will of the driver.

A very interesting combined gun-elevating and traversing gear, having no power assistance, is mounted in the turret.

Both the vehicles examined appear to have received little attention in service. Internally, however, the majority of parts were found to be in good condition, although severe wear had taken place in the cylinder bores and piston rings of both

Fig. 3. The head-on view shows the flat gun-mantlet, front driver's excape doors, vision slots and the W.T. aerial mounting on the turret.

engines, in relation to the small mileage recorded. This wear was due to sand passing through the air-cleaners.

The usual high standard of detail design, workmanship and foundry practice is evident in these vehicles. In our opinion, however, certain features are unfavourable to production, apart from the complication entailed by double-end control, and there appears to be scope for improving various characteristics of the design.

Fig. 2. Important features visible in this view are the front V-shaped shield carrying Notek headlamp (damaged), the numerous vision-ports and slots and the splash guard to driver's doors.

GENERAL DATA OF COMPLETE VEHICLE

Overall Dimensions.

Weight, with crew, service condition	17,640 lb.
Length	228.50 in.
Width	87.00 in.
Height	94.00 in.
Wheel Track (Axle shafts horizontal)	64.57 in.
Wheelbase (overall)	161.40 in.
„ (bogie)	53.15 in.
Bogie Centres	108.27 in.

Frame.

Section of side-member
    8.27 in. × 2.41 in. × 0.244 in.

Engine.

Make	Bussing-NAG.
Type	8-cylinder 90° V-Type, Petrol, O.H.V.
Capacity	7.91 litres
R.A.C. rating	56.79 H.P.
Max. B.H.P. (maker's rating)	155 at 3,000 r.p.m.
Max. torque (estimated)	361 lb. ft. at 1,500 r.p.m.

Clutch.

Type	Dry 2-plate
Outside diameter	10.945 in.
Total area of friction linings	245 sq. in.

Couplings.

(a) Engine—gearbox—axles   Jurid rubber-block type
(b) Final drive—wheels   Rzeppa type

Gearbox.

Type—Constant-mesh helical-gear.
Ratios—Six obtainable, forward or reverse.
Control—Two levers and one pedal, at each end of chassis.
Weight—(Dry and without mountings) 390 lb.

Final Drives.

Primary reduction	Helical spur gears, ratio 1.632 : 1
Secondary reduction	Spiral bevel gears, ratio 3.2 : 1
Overall ratio	5.222 : 1
Weight of intermediate axle, as shown in Fig. 33	910 lb.

Overall Ratios and Speeds

Speed	Overall Gear Ratios		Road Speed—m.p.h. at 3,000 r.p.m. of Engine	
	Forward	Reverse	Forward	Reverse
6th	6.06—1	5.95—1	50.1	50.99
5th	8.93—1	8.77—1	33.99	34.6
4th	15.97—1	15.72—1	19	19.32
3rd	21.05—1	20.63—1	14.42	14.72
2nd	31.02—1	30.50—1	9.79	9.95
1st	55.46—1	54.47—1	5.47	5.57

Table 1

Fig. 4. The chassis complete (except for engine and radiator) seen from the front, with the steering on full lock.

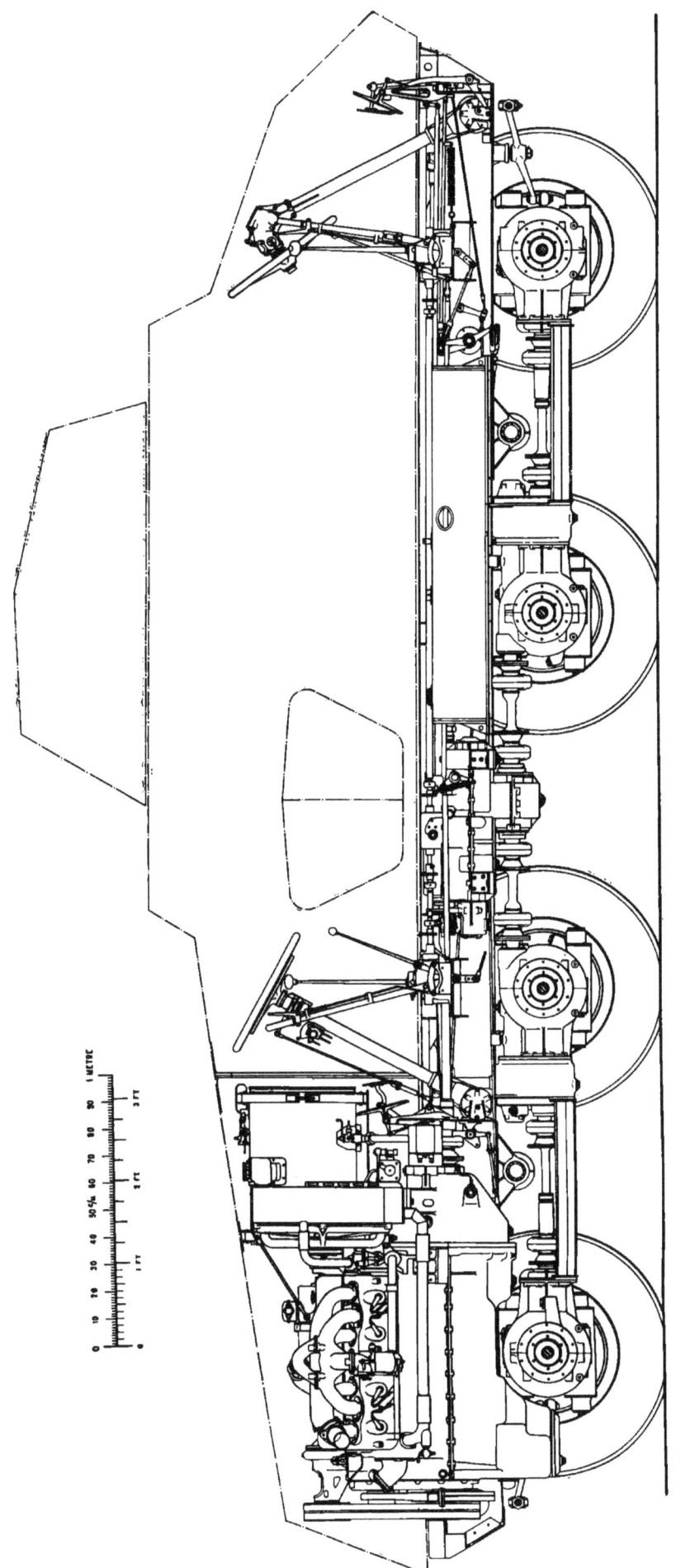

Fig. 5. A general arrangement of the chassis, in side elevation, showing also an outline of the hull.

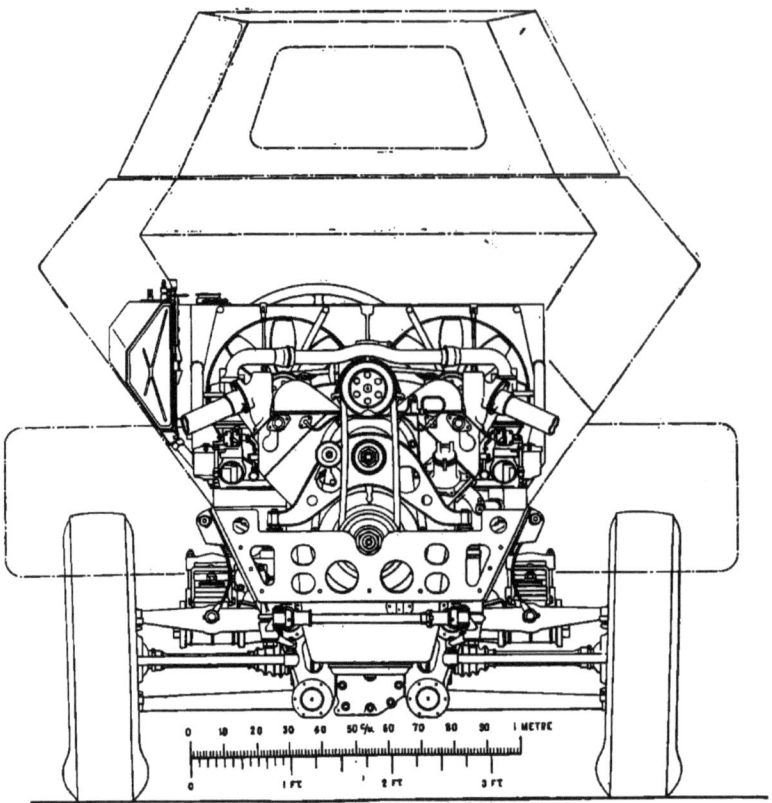

Fig. 6. A general arrangement of the chassis (rear elevation).

Tyres.
   Size   210 mm. × 18 in.
   Effective radius (static)
                    16.545 in. at 18% deflection
   Rolling radius (estimated)   17 in.
   Pressure   33 lb./sq. in. at 18% deflection

Suspension.
   Type   Semi-independent
   Springs   Leaf, inverted semi-elliptic
   Wheel rise, free to full load   4.77 in.
   Range of articulation, bumping to hanging   11.037 in.
   Ratio, sprung to unsprung weight   5.743 : 1

Steering Gear.
   Type   Worm and nut
   Maximum lock angle (wheel)   26°
   Turning circle diameter   449 in.
   Number of turns of wheel, lock to lock   4 front, 3½ rear

Brakes.
   Type   Wedge-expanded, two-shoe, full wrap
   Hook-up   Rods and cables
   Booster .. None
   Leverage, pedal-plate to shoe-centre .. 184 to 1
   Leverage, hand-grip to shoe-centre   354 to 1

Fuel System.
   Main tank capacity   24 gal. (Imp.)
   Auxiliary tank capacity   6.5 gal. (Imp.)

Electrical Equipment.
   Dynamo.. Bosch type GTL400/12-800 RS.37
                 12 volts : ventilated
                 Maximum output 600 watts
                 Speed 1.15 engine-speed

   Starter   Bosch type BNG4/24AL9
                 24 volts, axial shift
                 Drive—pinion 13 teeth
                           ring   134 teeth
   Ignition .. One Bosch impulse-type JO.8R5 magneto.

Chassis Lubrication.
   Type   Central supply
   Control .. Valve on steering column
   Feed from   Engine oiling system
   Feed to .. All steering connections, pedal and cross shafts, steering knuckles and vertical spindles and change-speed levers.

Armour Plates.
   Type   Surface hardened to Brinell 450-500.
   Joints   Faced and bolted junction of engine housing and main hull. All other joints welded.
   Thickness
      5 mm. Top plates of hull, engine housing and turret.
      8 mm. Front and sides of hull and turret
    10 mm. Sides and rear of engine housing
    15 mm. Gun mantlet

Armament.
One 2 cm. K.W.K.30 gun (or one 3.7 cm. Q.F. & S.A. gun) and one 7.90 mm. machine gun mounted co-axially in a flat mantlet and both fired by pedals on the gunner's foot-rest.

Ammunition.
2 cm.   180 rounds in magazines of 10 rounds
7.90 mm. 1,125 „   „   „   „ 75 rounds

Performance Factors.
Power/weight ratio 19.7 B.H.P. per ton (2,240 lb.)
Weight/power ratio 114 lb. per B.H.P.
Tractive Effort factors (100%) based on estimated torque—

(a) 6th gear ..   197 lb./ton (static)
(b) 1st gear   1,800 lb./ton (static)

FRAME

The chassis frame has two light "Z"-section side-members, parallel and of constant depth from end to end of the vehicle.

This chassis frame is, in effect, the assembly foundation for all components of the vehicle. Regarded purely as a load-carrying structure, it may be considered as largely redundant, its strength being negligible by comparison with the hull to which it is rigidly attached; for this reason, the frame is of very light construction. On the other hand, it performs a vital function, in that it enables all units to be assembled as a complete chassis with the same degree of accessibility as applies in the manufacture of a normal lorry, and, when assembled, the complete vehicle can be road-tested without the hull.

The advantages to the manufacturer of this feature must more than compensate for the apparently redundant weight of the frame. The adoption of a "Z"-section for the side-members appears to have been a very logical decision; the lower flanges of the channels are turned inwardly, so that the brackets used to suspend the final-drive gearboxes can be attached much more conveniently than would otherwise be the case. On the other hand, by turning the upper flanges outwardly, the designers have been enabled fully to utilise the space between the side-members to accommodate the gearbox, main fuel tank and other units which rest on the lower flanges, and therefore can be readily lifted out.

The main cross-members of the frame are really the two cross-tubes which extend under the side-members and form the pivots on which the four suspension springs rock. The attachment of these tubes to the side-members is shown in Fig. 41. In addition to these tubes, the four final-drive gearboxes, which are very rigidly attached to the side-members, also function as cross-members; this feature is illustrated in Fig. 37.

In addition to the above, six very light channel-section steel cross-members are provided, these serving principally to support the pedals and change-speed controls, etc. These auxiliary cross-members are all riveted to the side-members.

FRAME DIMENSIONS, Etc.	
Overall length of frame	5,560 mm.
Width of frame (outside webs) ..	544 mm.
Depth of side-members ..	210 mm.
Width of top flange	61.2 mm.
Width of bottom flange ..	61.2 mm.
Thickness of material	6.2 mm.
Outside dia. of bogie suspension tube	74 mm.
Inside dia. of bogie suspension tube	55 mm.

Table 2

Fig. 7. With the engine and radiator removed to expose details of construction and arrangement—a semi-plan, ¾ rear view of the chassis.

ENGINE

General Description

Maker : BUSSING-NAG.,
    Vereinigte Nutzkraft Wagen A.G., Leipzig.

The V-8 cylinder engine consists of two banks of four cylinders each, with an included angle of 90°, the right-hand bank (looking at the flywheel end) being offset forward relative to the left-hand bank. The connecting-rods are thus side by side on a common crankpin for each pair of cylinders.

The crankshaft, supported on three main bearings, of which the rear one takes the thrust, has a vibration-damper at the front end.

There are two valves per cylinder, mounted in the cylinder head and operated, through rockers, push-rods and round-based tappets, by a common camshaft, centrally disposed, and driven through a built-up composite (metal and fabric) idler gear, by a flexibly coupled helical-tooth pinion on the front end of the crankshaft.

At the rear end of the camshaft are the cam for operating the petrol lift-pump and the skew-gear drive for the Bosch magneto.

The gear-type oil pump, mounted on the front main bearing cap, is driven off the front end of the camshaft by skew gearing through a vertical extension of the pump shaft.

Pressure lubrication is provided for the main, big-end and valve-rocker bearings ; the camshaft runs in an oil-bath, and other items are lubricated by splash. A filter and a radiator are incorporated in the oil-system, and a tapping is taken off the main pressure-pipe for chassis lubrication.

The centrifugal water pump and the dynamo, mounted centrally above the camshaft, are driven in tandem by twin V-belts off the timing-gear end of the crankshaft. An extension-shaft, coupled to the dynamo, carries a twin pulley for two V-belts, each of which drives a radiator fan.

There are two Solex up-draught carburettors, one on each side of the cylinder block, connected to two separate oil-bath air-cleaners, and feeding into separate inlet manifolds, one for each bank of cylinders. These two manifolds are connected by a large-diameter balance-pipe across the top of the engine, and also by an internal passage cast in the cylinder heads and cylinder block.

The sparking plugs, one per cylinder, are screwed into the cylinder heads and project horizontally outwards, being fed from the magneto by screened leads.

Considerable detail differences, as set out in Table 3, were noticed between the engine fitted to the A.F.V. and that fitted to the A.C.V.

General Engine Data

Bore   107 mm.   4.2126 in.
Stroke   110 mm.   4.3307 in.
Capacity (one cylinder)
                       989.12 cc.   60.3598 cu. in.
Number of cylinders   8
Total capacity   7,912.96 cc.   482.8787 cu. in.
Compression ratio   5.5 : 1
Stroke/Bore ratio   1.03 : 1
Area of one piston
                  89.920 sq. cm.   13.9377 sq. in.
Total piston area   719.360 sq. cm.   111.5016 sq. in.
Max. b.h.p.   155
Max. r.p.m.   3,000
Mean piston speed at 3,000 r.p.m. 2,165 ft. per min.
Max. torque at 1,500 r.p.m.
   (estimated)   361 lb. ft.
Max. B.M.E.P. at 1,500 r.p.m.
   (estimated)   112.8 lb./sq. in.
Cylinder Numbering—
   Right-hand bank from flywheel end   7, 5, 3, 1
   Left-hand bank from flywheel end   8, 6, 4, 2
Direction of rotation
               Anti-clockwise from flywheel end
Firing order   1.2.7.3.4.5.6.8
Valve timing
     Inlet opens   14° before T.D.C.
     Inlet closes   58° after B.D.C.
     Exhaust opens 56° before B.D.C.
     Exhaust closes 16° after T.D.C.
Tappet clearance—at valve—inlet   .004 in.
                          —exhaust   .005 in.
Volume per b.h.p.   3.1153 cu. in.
Piston area per b.h.p.   .7194 sq. in.
B.h.p. per cu. ft.   553.39
B.h.p. per sq. ft. of piston area   200.18
Weight of engine complete (dry)   1,344 lb.
Weight per b.h.p.   8.67 lb.

Item	A.F.V.	A.C.V.
Engine No.	67186	67815
Cylinder Block :— Material	Cast-iron	Aluminium

Cylinder Liners :—
  Flange Location
  Sealing
  Outer coating
	Bottom
	Single flat joint
	Lead
		Top
		Two square rubber rings
		Nil

Cylinder Heads :—
  Combustion chamber
  Valve cover
	Fully machined
	Cast aluminium
		Partly machined
		Steel pressing

Main Bearing Caps :— Material	Cast-iron	Aluminium

Table 3

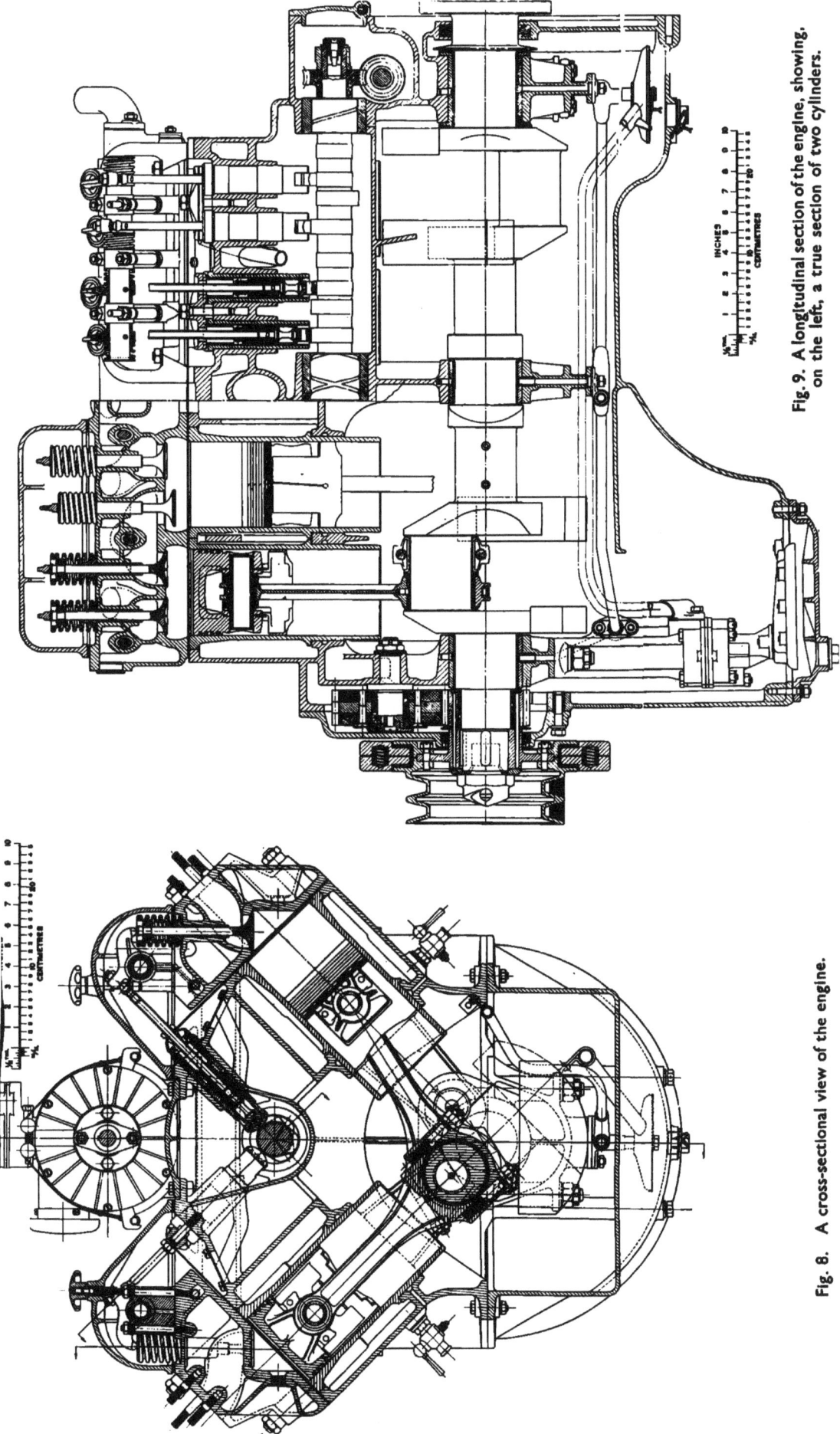

Fig. 9. A longitudinal section of the engine, showing, on the left, a true section of two cylinders.

Fig. 8. A cross-sectional view of the engine.

Detail Description of Engine No. 67186

(With variations for engine No. 67815)

CYLINDER BLOCK

The cylinder block is a monobloc iron casting, integral with the crankcase down to the centre line of the crankshaft. The wet cylinder liners, which are iron castings, lead-coated on the outside, are a light press-fit in the cylinder block. Each liner has, near its base, a flange which, with a thin flat joint, constitutes its seating. Below this, a leak-away groove

Fig. 10. The cylinder block (flywheel end). Note the induction balancing passage mentioned on pages 10 and 22.

is incorporated in the cylinder block. A water-tight joint at the top is maintained by the cylinder-head gasket. Water passages, to the inlet of the pump and from the outlet of the pump to the cylinder jackets, are cast integral with the cylinder block.

Cylinder-Block Dimensions	
Length—overall (bare block)	860 mm.
Length—centre to front	410 mm.
Length—centre to rear	450 mm.
C.L. of crankshaft to top of cylinders	365 mm.
Length—cylinder bore	236 mm.
Cylinder spacing—between pairs	134 mm.
Cylinder spacing—at centre	208 mm.
Cylinder offset—bank to bank	48 mm.
Angle between banks	90°

Table 4

Engine 67815.

This model exhibits the following variations from the above:—

The cylinder block is an aluminium casting. The cylinder liners are not lead-coated. They are located by a flange at the top and are sealed with two rubber ring joints at the bottom end, with a leak-away groove between them.

This cylinder block developed a crack, which appears to be caused by the liner sealing rings more than filling their grooves, thus exerting excessive radial pressure at this point and straining the block.

Flywheel Housing.

The flywheel housing is a separate aluminium casting, bolted to the rear face of the cylinder block.

Timing Gear Casing.

The timing-gear cover is also an aluminium casting; it extends below the centre-line of the crankshaft, and contains the crankshaft front oil-seal.

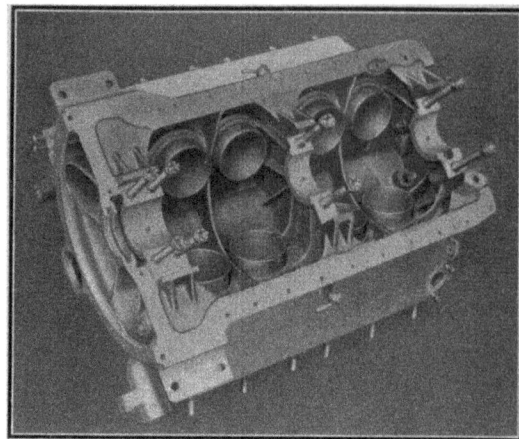

Fig. 11. This inverted semi-plan of the crankcase shows the helical strengthening webs. Note how the oil-pump drive-shaft entails off-set of the bearing-cap abutments and of one front bearing stud.

Suspension.

The front engine-bearer is a cross-member resting on the frame side-member, with rubber blocks interposed. It possesses a hollow boss, fabric-bushed internally, which accommodates a steel trunnion riveted to the timing-gear cover at camshaft height.

The rear suspension brackets are attached on each side of the cylinder block at the rear end, just above the centre-line of the crankshaft, and these also rest on rubber pads on the frame side-members.

CYLINDER HEADS.

The engine has two cast-iron cylinder heads, each covering four cylinders and fixed by studs and nuts, four per cylinder. The combustion chamber is fully machined, of 90° pent-roof shape, with the two valves in one side of the roof and the sparking plug (only one per cylinder) in the centre of the other side. The inlet ports are siamesed. The gasket is of compressed asbestos, reinforced by a steel insert.

Cylinder-Head Dimensions		
Port size—at valve	—inlet	42 mm.
	—exhaust	42 mm.
—at manifold	—inlet	42 mm.
	—exhaust	38 mm.
Cylinder-head stud :—		
Thread diameter		16 mm.
Waist diameter		11 mm.
Sparking plug size	18 mm. standard reach	

Table 5

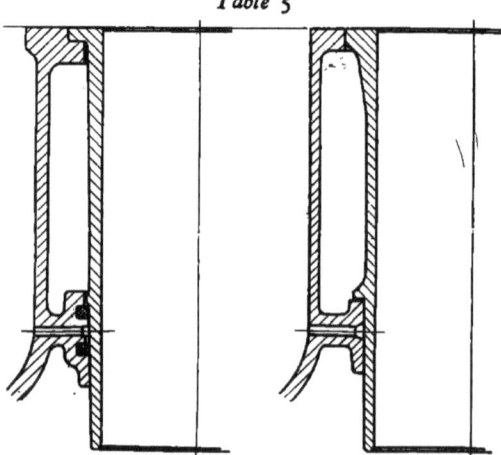

Fig. 12. Illustrating the different patterns of liners used in the two engines.

Engine 67815.
This model varies from the above in that the combustion chamber is only partly machined.

Pistons.

The pistons are aluminium alloy die castings, constructed on the lines of the Nelson patent—i.e. having steel inserts to control expansion. In this design, the flat head is attached only to the gudgeon-pin bosses, the skirt being fully cut away from the head, and slotted down to a point about 20 mm. from the base. Three compression rings and one grooved-and-slotted scraper ring are fitted, all above the gudgeon pin. The fully-floating gudgeon pin is retained by circlips.

Piston Dimensions

Nominal diameter	107 mm.
Overall length	123 mm.
Crown, above gudgeon pin	60 mm.
Skirt length	85 mm.
Skirt, above gudgeon pin	22 mm.
Width of ring grooves—compression	3.5 mm.
—scraper	5.0 mm.
Gudgeon pin—outside diameter	30.0 mm.
—inside diameter	22.0 mm.
—length	89.0 mm.

Piston Weights

Piston (bare)	2.195 lb.
Piston rings	0.195 lb.
Gudgeon pin	0.500 lb.
Total	2.890 lb.

Table 6

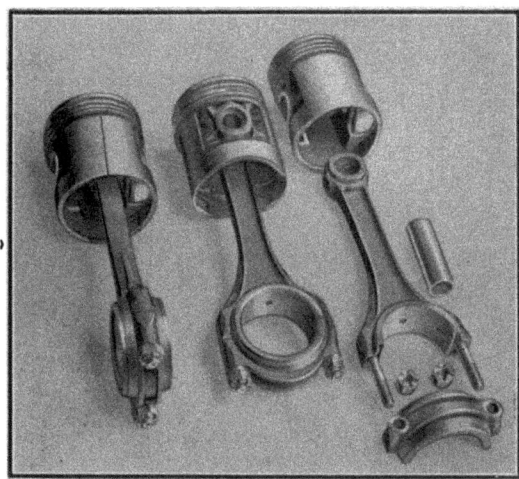

Fig. 14. Details of pistons and connecting-rods. Note the cylindrical register of the big-end caps.

The connecting-rod cap is a steel stamping, machined all over and located on the rod by a spigot in the joint face. The two studs for the cap are not screwed down completely in the rod, the rod and studs being cross-drilled and pinned to prevent rotation of the latter.

Note.—The connecting rod is too large to pass through the cylinder bore, and cannot be raised sufficiently to expose the gudgeon pin ; further, as the piston will not pass downwards between the crankshaft and the crankcase, if a piston has to be removed, the crankshaft must be taken out. This cannot be done with the engine in the chassis.

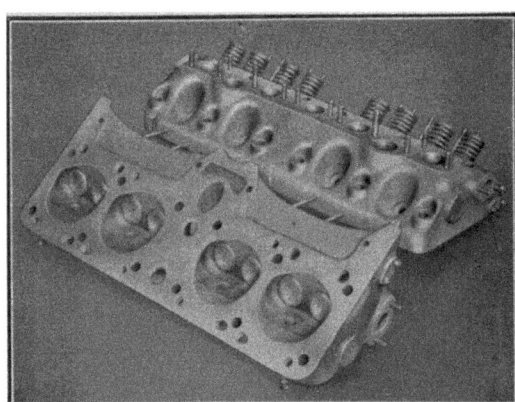

Fig. 13. Two aspects of the cylinder-head, showing machined combustion-chambers and the induction balancing passage with adjacent lightening cavity.

Connecting Rods.

The connecting rods are steel stampings machined all over, except the H section between the big and little ends. The little end is bronze bushed. The big-end bearings are steel-backed, with the lead-bronze lining carried right round the flanges of the bearing. Diametral location is provided by one dowel screwed into the rod.

Connecting-Rod Dimensions

Connecting-rod centres	245 mm.
H section—overall depth	32 mm.
—web thickness	3 mm.
—flange width	20 mm.
—flange thickness (at edge)	3 mm.
Little-end bearing, outside dia.	36 mm.
inside dia.	30 mm.
length (effective)	42 mm.
Big-end bearing, outside dia.	83 mm.
inside dia.	75 mm.
flange dia.	90 mm.
flange thickness	4 mm.
length, overall	46.5 mm.
effective	41 mm.
lining thickness	1.25 mm.
Cap studs—dia.	13 mm.
—centres	97 mm.

Connecting-Rod Weights
(Connecting rod complete with cap and bearings)

Little end	1.328 lb.
Big end	3.781 lb.
Total	5.109 lb.

Table 7

Fig. 15. This view of the crankshaft illustrates the disposition of the throws, and the asymmetrical form of the balance-weights.

CRANKSHAFT.

The four-throw crankshaft is a steel stamping, case-hardened on the crank-pins and journals, and machined all over. Balance-weights are attached to all crank webs (except those at the centre) by set bolts locked by tack welding.

The crank-pins are hollow, and closed by conical-seating caps at each end, with central retaining bolts. Oil-ways are drilled from the front journal to the first crank-pin, from the centre journal to the second and third crank-pins, and from the rear journal to the fourth crank-pin.

The vibration-damper is keyed to the front of the crankshaft and retained by the starting dog, which screws into the end of the crankshaft.

The timing-gear drive pinion, which is bronze bushed, floats on the crankshaft between the vibration-damper and the front main bearing. It has helical teeth and is connected to the crankshaft by 18 pins, the front ends of which are in the vibration-damper and their rear ends in the pinion. The holes accommodating these pins fit them for a short distance only at each end, but are gradually enlarged towards the middle of the pins, thus allowing a limited amount of rotational movement between the pinion and the crankshaft by flexure of the pins. The front oil-seal, of the spring-loaded lip type, is carried in the timing-gear cover. At the rear, there is an oil-flinger and an impregnated fabric ring for oil sealing, and the flywheel is attached by eight studs.

The crankshaft is carried in three main bearings, with cast-iron caps held to the crankcase by studs and split-pinned nuts. The rear bearing has large flanges to deal with end-thrust and the split line is not horizontal, being tilted approximately 3°. The reason for this tilt is not apparent. The bearings are steel-backed, with lead-bronze linings, and the top halves are located by one screwed-in dowel per bearing. The front and centre bottom halves are each located endwise by a hollow steel dowel, through which oil passes to the bearing.

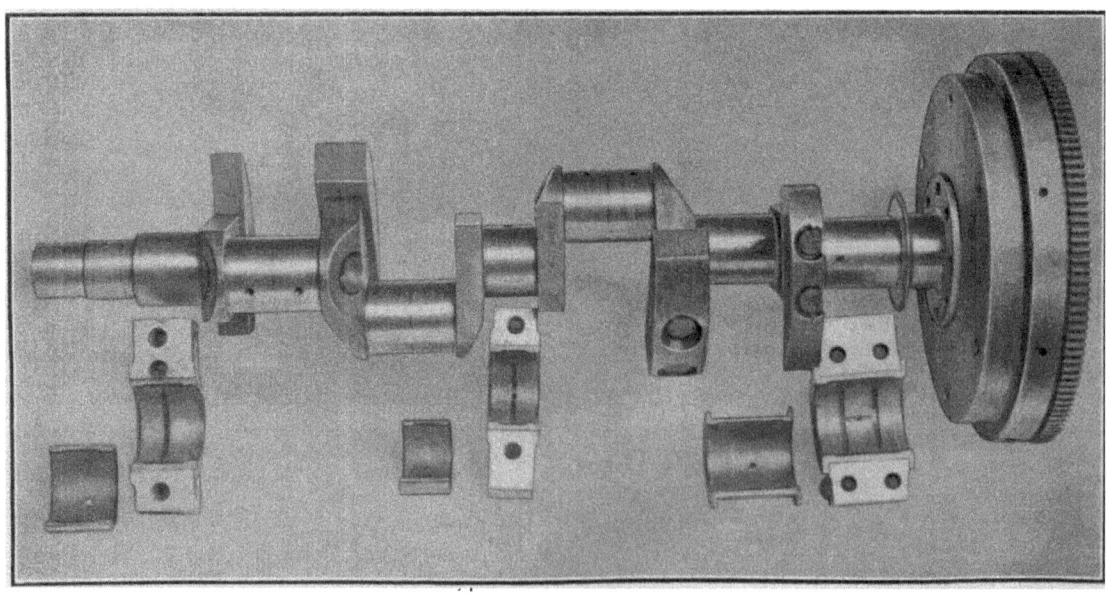

Fig. 16. A broadside view of the crankshaft, with bearings, caps and flywheel.

Crankshaft Dimensions

	Cranks	Front Journal	Centre Journal	Rear Journal
Pins.				
Diameter ..	75 mm.	75 mm.	75 mm.	75 mm.
Fillet radius	3 mm.	3 mm.	3 mm.	3 mm.
Length	93 mm.	69 mm.	56 mm.	94 mm.
Oil-hole diameter	5 mm.	10 mm.	10 mm.	10 mm.
Bearings.				
Outside diameter	83 mm.	90 mm.	90 mm.	90 mm.
Flange diameter ..	90 mm.	—	—	110 mm.
Flange thickness	4 mm.	—	—	6 mm.
Lining thickness	1.25 mm.	2 mm.	2 mm.	2 mm.
Effective length	41 mm.	61 mm.	47 mm.	85 mm.

	Front	Intermediate	Rear
Crank Webs.			
Thickness	28 mm.	40 mm.	28 mm.
Width	92 mm.	Triangular	92 mm.
Balance Weights.			
Thickness	33 mm.	55 mm.	33 mm.
Radius	125 mm.	125 mm.	125 mm.
Flywheel Studs.			
Diameter ..		16 mm.	
Number ..		8	
P.C. diameter		130 mm.	

	Front	Centre	Rear
Main Bearing Studs.			
Diameter ..	18 mm.	18 mm.	16 mm.
Number	2	2	4

Table 8

CAMSHAFT.

The camshaft is a steel stamping machined all over and case-hardened on the cam and bearing surfaces. It is carried on three bearings. A double-row ball bearing, with shim adjustment on its housing, locates the camshaft against end-thrust. The other two bearings are of bronze, and are a light press-fit in the cylinder block. Each is located and prevented from rotating by a screw dowel. The camshaft driving gear wheel, keyed to the front end of the camshaft, is an iron casting machined all over and having helical teeth. Behind the front bearing is the steel oil-pump driving gear, pressed on to the camshaft. Beyond the rear bearing, the bronze magneto driving gear and the case-hardened steel cam for operating the petrol lift-pump are both keyed on the camshaft and retained by a set-screw in the camshaft end. This set-screw has two longitudinal saw-cuts at right angles and is tapped internally to accommodate a threaded pin; when tightened up, the end of this, being tapered, expands and locks the set-screw.

The idler gear, between the camshaft and the crankshaft, is of laminated construction. It consists of three layers, mounted on a bronze centre and

Fig. 17. Timing cover and bearer-arm have been detached to expose the timing train with drive by multiple spring pins.

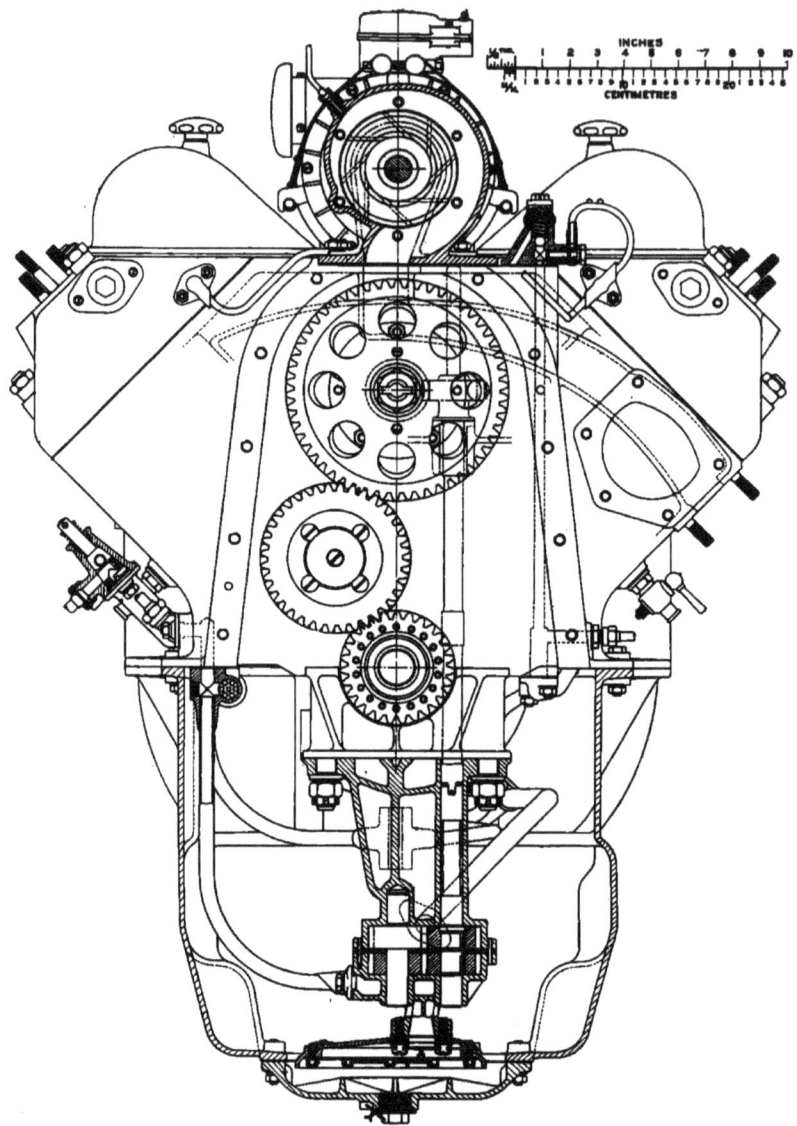

Fig. 18. Front end elevation of the engine, with timing cover removed, showing also (in section) water pump, oil pump, pressure-release valve and oil-cooler isolating valve.

held, between the flange on the centre and a circular retaining plate, by four countersunk-head set-screws. The central layer is aluminium, and the outer layers are of a compressed impregnated fabric similar to Fabroil.

VALVE GEAR.

Two valves per cylinder are fitted, the exhaust being identical with the inlet. They are of semi-tulip

Camshaft Dimensions			
General diameter of shaft		42	mm.
Centre bearing, outside dia.		80	mm.
Centre bearing, inside dia.		60	mm.
Effective length of centre bearing		58	mm.
Rear bearing, outside dia.		80	mm.
Rear bearing, inside dia.		56	mm.
Effective length of rear bearing		41	mm.
Cam—bottom radius		22	mm.
—effective lift*		7.47	mm.
—effective width		16	mm.
	Width	P.C. Dia.	No. of teeth
Camshaft gear	45 mm.	201	54
Idler gear	44 mm.	134	36
Crankshaft pinion	45 mm.	100.5	27
* See also Table 11.			

Table 9

Fig. 19. Detail of valve operation, showing attachment of ball-cups to push-rods, and the cover-facing on head and block.

Valve-Gear Dimensions

Valves.
- Lift .. 10.5 mm.
- Head diameter 46 mm.
- Port diameter 42 mm.
- Seat angle 30°
- Stem diameter .. 10 mm.
- Diameter at collet 8 mm.
- Overall length 142 mm.

Valve Guide.
- Length .. .. 80 mm.
- Outside diameter 15 mm.
- Inside diameter 10 mm.

Rockers.
- Arm length—to valve .. 45 mm.
- —to push-rod 32 mm.
- Bearing —length .. 34 mm.
- —inside diameter 25 mm.
- —outside diameter 28 mm.
- Width of pad .. 11 mm.
- Diameter of set-screw 10 mm.

Push-rods.
- Tube—outside diameter 10 mm.
- —overall length 220 mm.

Tappets.
- Outside diameter 24 mm.
- Inside diameter 20 mm.
- Effective length 67 mm.
- Base radius 20 mm.
- Base width 16 mm.

Springs	Valve Spring, Outer	Valve Spring, Inner	Push-rod Spring
Mean diameter	35 mm.	25 mm.	15.5 mm.
Wire diameter ..	.176 in. (7 SWG)	.128 in. (10 SWG)	.104 in (12 SWG)
Effective number of coils	6	7	15
Free length ..	66 mm.	55 mm.	77 mm.
Working length	54 mm.	41.5 mm.	59 mm.
Closed length	31 mm.	26 mm.	42 mm.
Rate	108 lb./in.	54 lb./in.	42 lb./in.

Valve-Gear Weights

- Valve .. .328 lb.
- Spring (outer) .. .234 lb.
- Spring (inner) .. .094 lb.
- Spring cap .094 lb.
- Collet .. .023 lb.
- End pad .008 lb.
- Push-rod .172 lb.
- Spring .070 lb.
- Tappet .. .. .281 lb.
- Rocker (valve arm) .. .096 lb. ⎱ estimated
- Rocker (push-rod arm) .100 lb. ⎰ equivalent

Table 10

CAM CHARACTERISTICS

Angle from Peak	Tappet Lift	Change in Lift
68°	− .003″*	
		.002″
65°	− .001″	
		.001″
63°	.000″	
		.0025″
60°	.0025″	
		.010″
55°	.0125″	
		.018″
50°	.0305″	
		.028″
45°	.0585″	
		.040″
40°	.0985″	
		.044″
35°	.1425″	
		.042″
30°	.1845″	
		.0375″
25°	.222″	
		.0295″
20°	.2515″	
		.022″
15°	.2735″	
		.012″
10°	.2855″	
		.003″
5°	.2885″	
		.001″
0°	.2895″	
		.001″
5°	.2885″	
		.003″
10°	.2855″	
		.012″
15°	.2735″	
		.022″
20°	.2515″	
		.0295″
25°	.222″	
		.0375″
30°	.1845″	
		.042″
35°	.1425″	
		.044″
40°	.0985″	
		.040″
45°	.0585″	
		.028″
50°	.0305″	
		.018″
55°	.0125″	
		.010″
60°	.0025″	
		.0025″
63°	.000″	
		.001″
65°	−.001″	
		.002″
68°	−.003″*	

Inlet and exhaust cams are identical. Tappet bases have a 20 mm. radius. The interval between exhaust and inlet cams is 111°.
* Tappet clearance.

Table 11

type with a screw-driver slot in the head. Two coil springs are fitted to each valve. The general design of the rocker-gear is quite orthodox, the adjustment being carried out by a spherically ended screw at the push-rod end of each rocker. Above the spherical base of each tubular push-rod is formed a collar on which bears a return spring housed inside the tubular tappet body and retained, at its upper end, by the clamp that retains the cast-iron tappet guide. Each case-hardened tappet has a cylindrically-faced foot, the sides of which slide in slots in the tappet guide to prevent rotation. Slight indentation had taken place at the point of contact with the cam.

Each group of four valves and rockers is enclosed by a cast-aluminium cover, held on by two retaining hand-grip nuts. A thick cork joint is used, as the cover seats partly on the cylinder head and partly on the cylinder block.

Engine 67815.

This model has valve-rocker covers in pressed steel instead of cast aluminium.

OIL PUMP AND LUBRICATION SYSTEM.

The system employs a wet sump of cast aluminium exactly the same length as the cylinder block, with the lower portions of the front cover and the flywheel housing bolting on to it at the front and the rear respectively. The main reservoir, or deep section of the sump, is at the opposite end to the flywheel, and contains the submerged oil-pump. To avoid oil starvation on severe gradients, a secondary sump is formed at the other end; this is evacuated through a suction-pipe by a scavenge-pump discharging into the main reservoir. A diagrammatic layout of the system is shown in Fig. 20.

The oil pump, mounted on the front main bearing cap, is a gear pump with two compartments. The

---

Oil-Pump Dimensions, Etc.

Oil-pump speed	½ engine speed
Scavenge pump—gear outside dia.	55 mm.
—root dia.	44 mm.
—number of teeth	20
—width of teeth	22 mm.
Pressure pump—gear outside dia.	55 mm.
—root dia.	44 mm.
—number of teeth	20
—width of teeth	20 mm.

Estimated 100 per cent. capacity of pump at 1,000 r.p.m. (engine).
Scavenge-pump   2.07 gal. (Imp.) per min.
Pressure-pump   1.88 gal. (Imp.) per min.

Table 12

---

body and cover are aluminium castings, with a dividing plate of bronze interposed between the two; body, plate and cover are located together by two dowels. The upper compartment contains the scavenge pump, and the lower compartment contains the main pump.

The oil pump appears to be rather small in relation to the bearing sizes; when the engine is hot, oil pressure is between 100 and 140 lb. per sq. in. at high speed but falls to about 20 lb. per sq. in. at idling speed.

From the main oil reservoir at the front the oil is drawn up, through a gauze filter, by the main pump, and its path from this point onwards is clearly shown in the accompanying diagram (Fig. 20).

The function of the two-way tap in the connections to the filter and radiator is to enable the oil to be short-circuited past the filter and radiator, presumably in case of damage to the circuit containing these components.

rocker-brackets, and feeds, by means of drilled passages in the inner rocker-brackets, to the hollow rocker-shafts, and thence, by holes in the latter, to the rocker bearings. A drilled hole in each rocker is fed from the rocker bearings and directs an oil jet into the cup of the push-rod. Surplus oil from the valve-gear is drained off to the camshaft oil-bath, which has a level-hole at the front end, through which oil spills on to the timing gear.

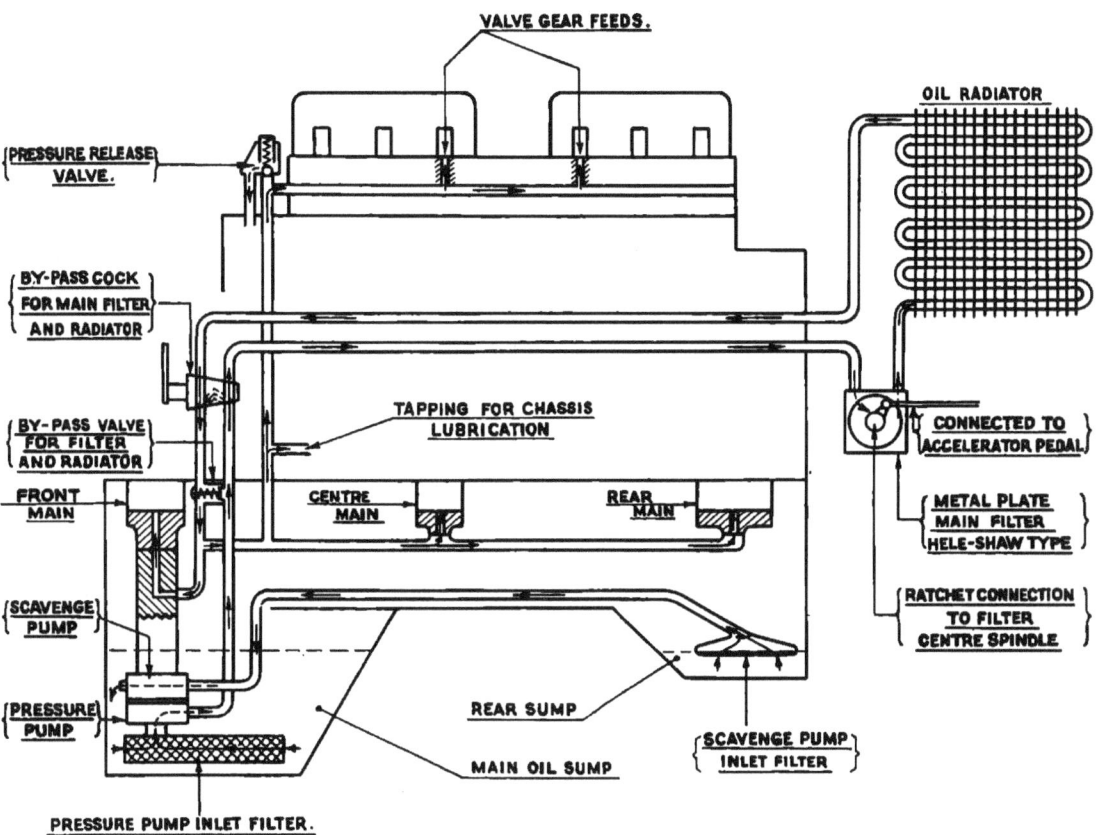

Fig. 20. A diagram which illustrates the course of the oil through the engine and radiator.

The filter and radiator by-pass valve is of the disc type, with 45° seat-angle, allowing full flow of oil in the event of the external circuit becoming clogged.

The adjustable oil-pressure release-valve, mounted on the top of the cylinder block at the front end, seems to be of very small size (10 mm. dia. ball). The overflow from this valve feeds into the camshaft oil-bath.

The valve-gear feed-pipe is coupled from this valve across to an oil pipe pressed into each cylinder head. This oil pipe passes along underneath the

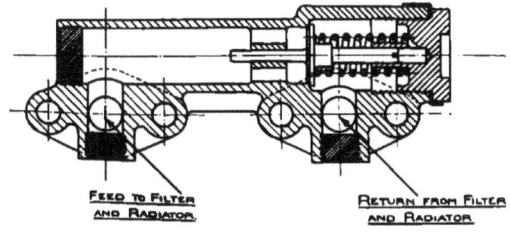

Fig. 21. A sectional view of the oil by-pass valve.

The camshaft idler-gear spindle is lubricated by a trough on the back of the wall to which it is mounted, the oil collected passing through drilled holes to the front and thus to the spindle.

All other parts of the engine are lubricated by splash or mist.

WATER PUMP AND COOLING SYSTEM.

The water pump, located in the V between the cylinders, is of centrifugal design, but with straight blades. The bronze rotor is pressed and pinned on to a stainless-steel shaft, which is supported at the front end by a double-row ball bearing just behind the driving pulley, and at the rear end by a bronze bush in the pump cover. The pump body and cover are light alloy castings. The pump is sealed by a spring-loaded, synthetic rubber, lip-type seal on each side of the rotor, each backed by a felt ring. Each seal is fed with oil from an oil cup, and the oil is retained by another lip-type oil seal placed farther along the pump shaft.

The radiator, which is mounted at the flywheel end of the engine, has air circulated through it by two belt-driven fans. The water outlet pipe from the radiator passes along the left-hand bank of

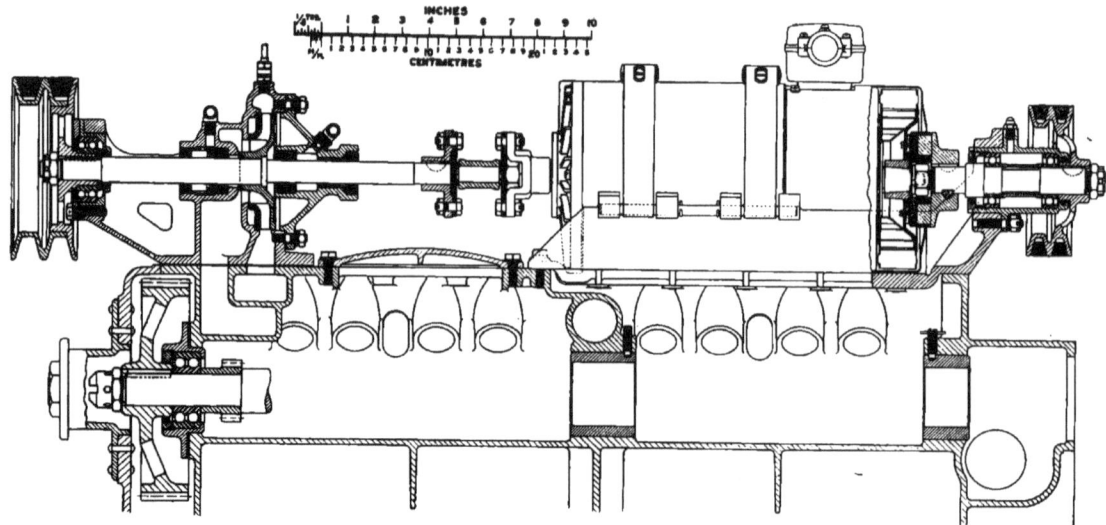

Fig. 22. A section through the auxiliary drive and camshaft tunnel. Belts from the right-hand pulley drive the fans.

cylinders to the front of the cylinder block, where an elbow connects it with the cast-in passage to the pump inlet.

The pump outlet feeds both cylinder banks through cast-in passages at the front end, and the water passes up through the cylinder-head joints to the heads. Thence it passes to the rear of the heads, where outlet elbows connect with the radiator header-tank. Owing to the high position of the water pump, a small-diameter pipe leads from the top of the pump to the radiator header-tank, to carry away any air trapped in the pump after draining and refilling the cooling system.

Water-Pump Dimensions, Etc.	
Water pump speed	1.15 engine speed
Rotor—outlet dia.	.. 110 mm.
—outlet width ..	9 mm.
—inlet outside dia.	60 mm.
—inlet inside dia.	36 mm.
Rotor shaft dia.	24 mm.

Table 13

Fig. 23. The flywheel end of the complete engine. Note the unusual starter location, the fan-driving pulley and the magneto.

Fig. 24. A ¾ view of the complete engine (timing-gear end), showing ignition cut-out governor driven from the camshaft end, and the large manifold balancing-pipe arched over the dynamo.

Induction and Exhaust System

The two carburettors were removed from the engine and sent to Messrs. Solex Ltd. for examination; the following report was received:—

"These carburettors are similar to our type 46 MOVSL.

"Like these, they are made of two main sand castings; one of them forms the float chamber and the other combines the float chamber cover and the throttle tube. They are fitted with an ordinary self-starter, no special provision being made on the carburettor to help starting in very cold weather. The butterfly is our old bossed type, and the jet system is our old No. 6 Assembly.

"The only differences with our 46 MOVSL. carburettor refer to minor details.

"The float chamber has the air-intake pointing sideways and this has led to a modification of the usual boss carrying the jet well. In its normal form this boss would have caused a serious obstruction to the air entering the carburettor and a swirl detrimental to good distribution. The solid boss has therefore been replaced by a cast central pillar linked at the top to the wall of the air intake by an arm extending horizontally. The central pillar is used to convey the petrol from the float chamber to the jet well, and the lateral arm is used for the petrol feeding the slow-running jet.

"In carburettor No. IC.6172, behind the central pillar and on the centre line of the air intake is drilled a 12 mm. hole through the air intake well. This has probably been done to overcome some distribution defect. This hole is not drilled in carburettor No. IX.4957.

"The float chamber mechanism is the same as in our 46 MOVSL. carburettor, but the float has an unusual weight, 67 gr. and no special care has been taken to round off the edges of its central tube. Also provision has been made in the float-chamber cover for the fitting of the needle valve in three alternative positions, each corresponding to a different petrol connection on the side of the cover. The banjo union may therefore be fitted either axially, as in our 46 MOVSL. carburettor, or on either side of the float-chamber cover.

"The main jet itself is not our usual type, but embodies a principle which we have occasionally used, as at Leyland, i.e. the calibrated orifice forms a separate member independent of the emulsifying tube. The main jet is screwed direct into the bottom of the float chamber, and the petrol issuing from it reaches the lower end of the central pillar through two channels drilled round the outside of the air intake. This arrangement has probably been adopted to reduce the danger of vapour lock.

"In the top of the jet cap a small hole has been drilled through one of the flats of the hexagon, the object of which appears to break a tendency for the petrol to syphon over the edge of the jet well. It is not clear, however, why such a tendency should prevail.

"In the throttle tube itself nothing really new could be detected. It was, however, noticed that, although a gun-metal casting, it was very yellow in colour, looking, in fact, just like brass where the metal skin has been removed.

"The float chamber casting is good quality aluminium.

"The carburettors are not dust-proof in any way, but both were in good condition and they have been re-assembled with their original parts except the throttle spindles which had to be replaced as the butterfly screws had to be drilled out, they having become rusted in position.

"The setting used in both carburettors was:—

		IX.4957	IC.6172
Choke tube	30		
Main jet	145 flowing	142 c.c.	142 c.c.
Pilot jet	55 flowing	57 c.c.	58 c.c.
Needle valve	2.0		
G.A.	4.5 × 2		
G.S.	200 flowing	170 c.c.	170 c.c.

Float similar to No. 50572 but weighs 67 gr.
Jet cap similar to No. 4661/1 but having 1.5 hole in flat of top hexagon.
Emulsion tube as main jet 4730/61 but bored 4.2 mm. right through, overall height 38.5 mm. instead of 39.2 mm. and bottom holes drilled at 3.5 mm. from bottom instead of 4.7 mm.
Jet stand as No. 4659 but bored 10 mm. instead of 9.5 mm.
Pilot jet as No. 50552/5.
Starter jet as No. 50676 but with 2 lateral holes 1.4 mm. dia.
Air jet as No. 50906.
Starter valve as No. 50979.
Starter body No. 51426, emulsion tube projecting 61.5 and 2.2 mm. hole drilled 5 mm. from bottom.
Throttle No. 4320/C with 1.45 mm. vent hole at 9 mm. from centre line of spindle towards boss.
Choke tube No. 4318.
Throttle spindle No. 50571.
Air regulating screw No. 4826.
Needle seating No. 51305/7.
Starter on L/H side looking at float chamber.
Starter lever away from float chamber, and up to flange to operate.
Air intake pointing to L/H. side looking at float chamber on carburettor No. IC.6172 and to R/H. side on carburettor No. IX.4957.

"On carburettor No. IX.4957 a throttle lever is fitted over the float chamber, attached to the spindle by the usual double D-shaped slot and with a 10 mm. ball at 42 mm. from centre line of spindle.

"On carburettor No. IC.6172 no throttle lever is fitted.

"On both carburettors the abutment plate is fitted on the end of the spindle away from the float chamber.

"On both carburettors the petrol connection is fitted to the R/H. side looking at float chamber."

Each carburettor draws air through an oil-bath filter and feeds mixture into an individual cast-aluminium manifold attached to the outside of its respective cylinder head. The manifolds are connected across the top of the engine by a large-diameter pipe and also by passages cast in the cylinder heads and block. There is no hot-spot in the manifold system, the induction manifolds being separated from the exhaust manifolds by asbestos-lined shields. Two separate exhaust pipes lead into two box-type silencers, one attached above each rear mudguard.

Induction Dimensions

Section	Diameter	Area in sq. cm.	Gas Velocity in f.p.s. at 1,000 r.p.m.
Choke	30 mm. less 16 mm.	5.058	213.6
Carburettor	48 mm.	18.096	59.8
Manifold Entry	49 mm.	18.857	57.3
Manifold Branch	41 mm.	13.203	81.8
Manifold Exit	41 mm.	13.203	81.8
Cylinder Head Entry	42 mm.	13.854	78.2
Valve Port	42 mm. less 10 mm.	13.069	82.8
Balance pipe, inside diameter		36 mm.	
Balance passage, inside diameter		40 mm.	

Table 14

CLUTCH

In each vehicle, the clutch is enclosed by a casing bolted to the engine flywheel housing and provided with ventilation openings; these have no special provision for exclusion of dirt or water.

Both clutches are entirely conventional, with the exception of the bearings of the internal levers in the Fichtel & Sachs clutch.

These bearings are of the needle type. Although no provision has been made for the lubrication of these bearings, the needles had become only slightly rusted.

Considerable differences exist between the clutch fitted to the Armoured Fighting Vehicle and that of the Armoured Command Vehicle.

These differences and other leading particulars of these clutches are given in the adjoining column.

	A.F.V.	A.C.V.
Make of clutch	Fichtel & Sachs	Long
Number of acting surfaces	4	
O.D. of friction lining	278 mm.=10.945 in.	
I.D. of friction lining	164 mm.= 6.44 in.	
Total friction surface	245 sq. in.	
Internal levers	Stamped	Pressed
Clutch cover	Cast	Pressed
Internal leverage	4.36 : 1	5.4 : 1
External leverage	5.05 : 1	4.75 : 1
Total leverage, pedal to presser plate	22.0 : 1	25.6 : 1
Clutch brake	None	None

COUPLING SHAFTS

Short solid shafts, having joints of Jurid make, couple all units of the transmission to each other, and to the engine.

These joints, the construction of which is shown in Fig. 27, are similar to the type introduced into England under the name of "Powerflex."

In this type, each of the driving and driven elements consists of a hub having two oppositely-spaced arms; in the assembled joint, the driving arms are held at 90° to the driven arms by segmental rubber blocks which transmit the drive. The two halves of the coupling are held concentric by a ball-and-socket joint. As all units are mounted on the frame and relatively aligned, these joints have to accommodate negligible angularity.

When dismantled, the engine-to-gearbox couplings were already beginning to disintegrate, but the remaining couplings, in which the stresses are progressively reduced as higher gears are engaged, appeared intact. Particulars of joint loading are given in Table 15.

Coupling Dimensions and Loadings			
	Position of Coupling		
	Engine to Gearbox	Gearbox to Axles	Axle to Axle
Mean radius of rubber block in.	1.67	2.05	2.05
Bearing area of two blocks .. sq. in.	1.87	2.75	2.75
Maximum torque, 1st gear .. lb. ft.	361	1,917	1,560
Maximum torque, top gear .. .. lb. ft.	361	180	147
Bearing pressure on rubber blocks, 1st gear, lb. per sq. in.	1,387	4,080	3,330
Bearing pressure on rubber blocks, top gear, lb. per sq. in.	1,387	384	313

Table 15

GEARBOX

The gearbox is a separate unit mounted amidships in the frame on four flat rubber pads resting on the lower flanges of the " Z "-section side-members.

Essentially, it is a three-speed gearbox incorporating an auxiliary high-low ratio of 3.47 : 1 and thereby affording six distinct ratios by the use of two gear levers. A heel-and-toe pedal controls forward or reverse motion, and all speeds are available in either direction.

The main and auxiliary gear levers, and the reverse pedal, are duplicated, one set being provided at each end of the vehicle.

There is no provision for synchro-mesh, but an attempt has been made to facilitate the high-low shift by providing a spring-loaded coupling in between the auxiliary shift lever and its associated dog-clutches, which are of the type made familiar by the Maybach Company.

The gearbox has four shafts enabling the drive to drop successively from the level of the crankshaft to that of the final-drive input shaft, and consequently even with the highest ratio, the drive is transmitted through four gears in the forward direction and two additional gears are brought into play in reverse. This accounts for the large number of gear-wheels (14), and it is noteworthy that, in the lowest speed, the drive is taken through no less than 10 gear-wheels in the forward direction. Twelve of the gear-wheels have helical teeth and are in constant mesh; the two used for first and fourth speeds have straight teeth.

Great pains have been taken to provide bearings close to each gear-wheel and four have a bearing each side. This has necessitated splitting the gearbox casing through the shaft centre-line, and the casing is therefore in four sections requiring a considerable number of tapered dowels, studs and bolts.

There are no less than 26 bearings of various

REVERSE ← DIRECTION OF TRAVEL

SPEED	RATIO	STEPS	GEAR SEQUENCE		REAR SEAT CONTROLS HAND & FOOT
6TH	1·14-1	1·47	DC. FE. KJ.	HIGH RATIO 1-1	
5TH	1·68-1	1·79	DC. BA. KJ.		
4TH	3·01-1	1·31	DC. IH. KJ.		
3RD	3·95-1	1·48	DC. FE. MN. LKJ.	LOW RATIO 3·47-1 REDUCTION	
2ND	5·84-1	1·79	DC. BA. MM. LKJ.		
1ST	10·43-1		DC. IH. MN. LKJ.		

RATIO OF FORWARD TO REVERSE 1·018-1

FORWARD DIRECTION OF TRAVEL →

SPEED	RATIO	STEPS	GEAR SEQUENCE		FRONT SEAT CONTROLS HAND & FOOT
6TH	1·16-1	1·47	GE. KJ.	HIGH RATIO 1-1	
5TH	1·71-1	1·79	GEF. BA. KJ.		
4TH	3·06-1	1·31	GEF. IH. KJ.		
3RD	4·03-1	1·48	GE. MN. LKJ.	LOW RATIO 3·47-1 REDUCTION	
2ND	5·94-1	1·79	GEF. BA. MN. LKJ.		
1ST	10·62-1		GEF. IH. MN. LKJ.		

Fig. 25. A diagram of gear-change positions showing how the different ratios are obtained.

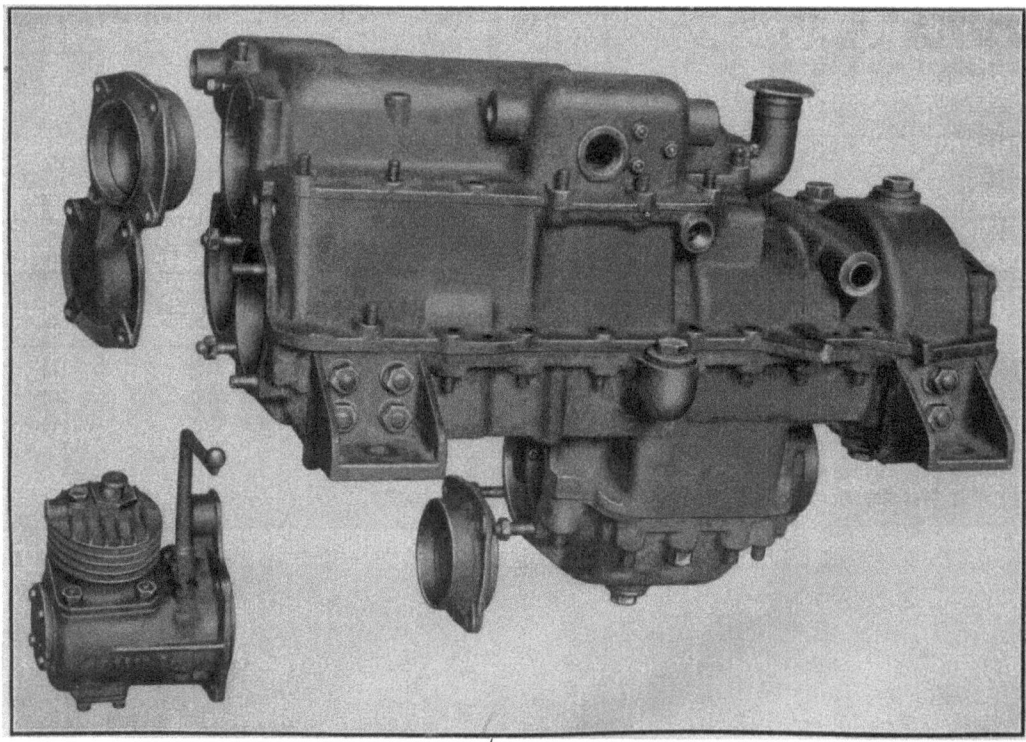

Fig. 26. The gearbox casing consists of the four main castings here seen with the tyre-pump and two bearing-housings detached.

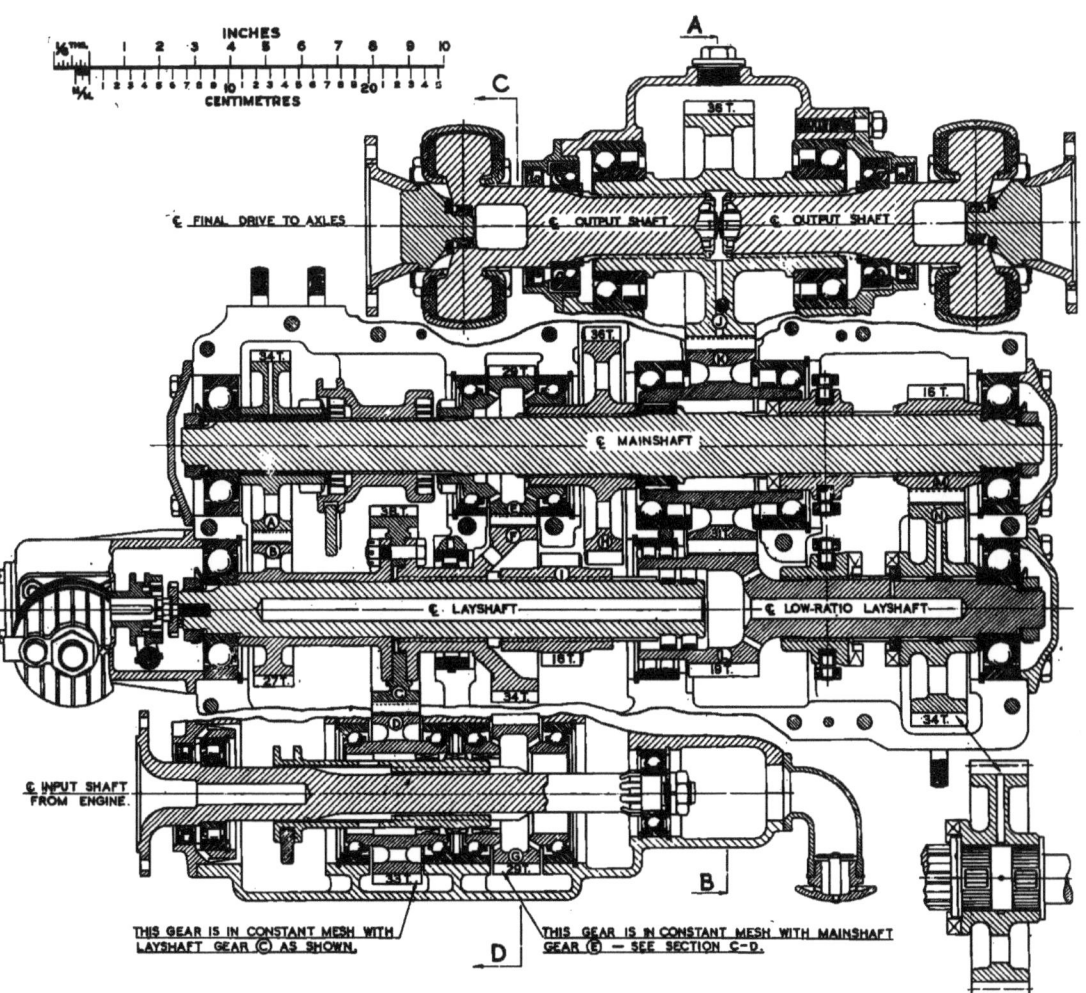

Fig. 27. A developed longitudinal section of the gearbox. For true relative positions of shafts, see Figs. 28 and 29.

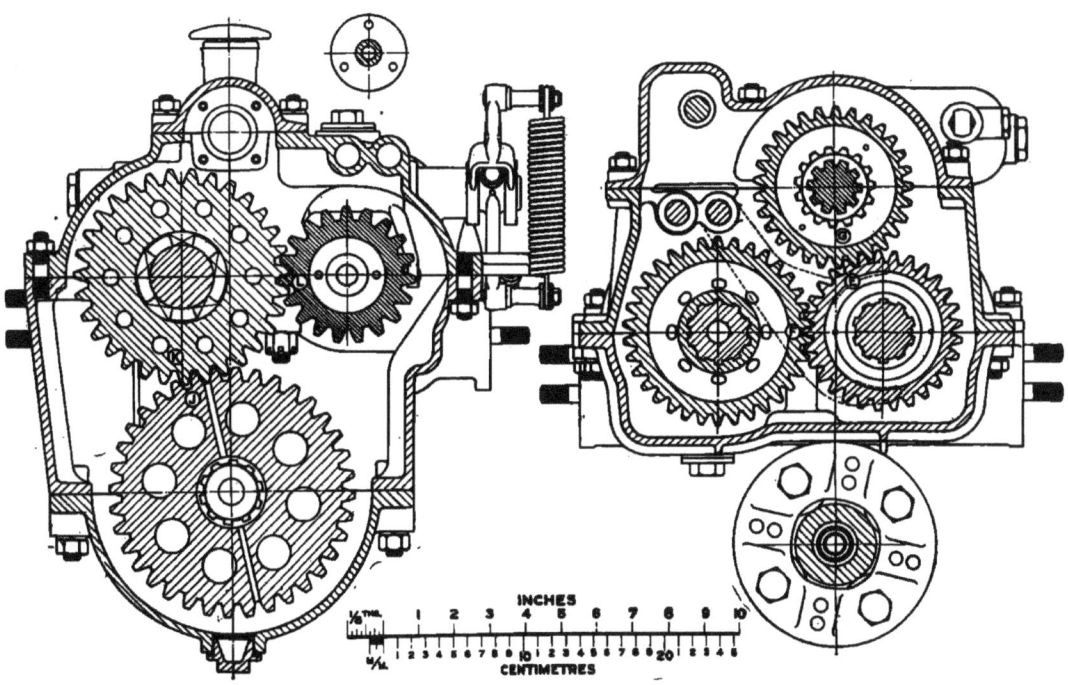

Fig. 28. A cross-section of the gearbox through AB. (See Fig. 27.)

Fig. 29. A cross-section of the gearbox through CD. (See Fig. 27.)

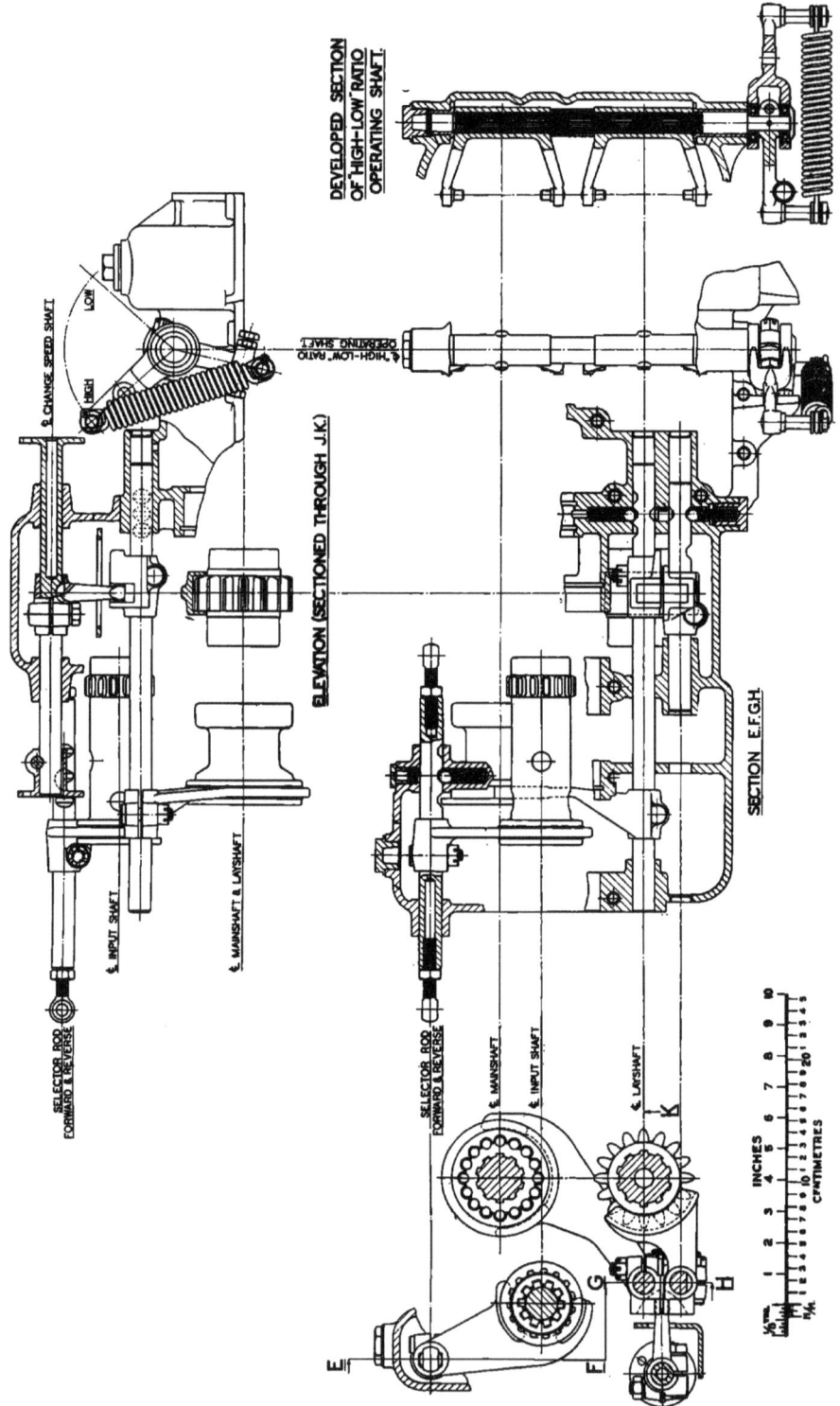

Fig. 30. Arrangement of the gearbox selector mechanism.

Fig. 31. An interior view of the gearbox casing, displaying the large number of bearing-seatings.

types in the gearbox, and in many cases space-requirements have necessitated forming the tracks integral with the gears. In some cases four bearing tracks have been machined on the hub of one gear-wheel, two for roller and two for ball bearings.

Lack of space between the mainshaft and layshaft has necessitated grinding grooves in the outer races of some bearings to accommodate a stud. This operation appears to have been carried out by the gearbox makers, thereby rendering the bearing non-standard.

Four other bearings are worthy of comment on account of their unusual construction. In this type, each race has both roller and ball tracks, and whilst the row of balls is contained in a cage, no cage is provided for the rollers.

A single-cylinder tyre pump 50 mm. bore × 30 mm. stroke is mounted on the engine end of the gearbox casing and is driven by a sliding dog engaging directly with the end of the layshaft.

When stripped, all parts of the gearbox were found to be in good condition, excepting the spur gears used for first and fourth speeds. These gears have to slide into mesh and showed considerable wear on the engaging ends of the teeth.

Full gear particulars and tooth loadings are shown in Table 16. The various ratios with the corresponding positions of the controls are shown in Fig. 25.

GEARBOX GEAR DATA

Gear	Number of Teeth	Effective Tooth Width mm.	Angle of Pressure	Module	Spiral Angle	Length of Lead mm.	Hand	Outside Dia. mm.	Pitch Dia. mm.	Max. Tooth Loading.* (lb. per in. width of race)	Rockwell Hardness at—			
											Teeth	Dogs	Bearing Tracks	Splines
A	34	28	20°	3½	24° 9' 43"	914.36	R.H.	137.43	130.43	2,269	C 60	C 60		
B	27	28	20°	3½	24° 9' 43"	726.61	L.H.	110.57	103.57	2,269	C 59			
C	38	34	20°	3½	19° 49' 39"	1,233.32	L.H.	148.38	141.38	1,337	C 60			
D	33	34	20°	3½	19° 49' 39"	1,071.04	R.H.	129.78	122.78	1,337	C 56		C 60	
E	29	34	20°	3½	19° 33' 26"	953.34	R.H.	114.71	107.71	1,526	C 55	C 59	C 58	C 59
F	34	34	20°	3½	19° 33' 26"	1,117.73	L.H.	133.29	126.29	1,526	C 59		C 55	
G	29	34	20°	3½	19° 33' 26"	953.34	L.H.	114.71	107.71	1,526	C 59		C 59	
H	36	24	22° 30'	4½	Straight Spur			171.00	162.00	3,791	C 60			
I	16	24	22° 30'	4½	Straight Spur			81.00	72.00	3,791	C 60§			C 60
J	36	50	20°	4½	15° 56' 33"	1,855.12	L.H.	177.48	168.48	7,044	C 59			C 61
K	31	50	20°	4½	15° 56' 33"	1,597.47	R.H.	154.08	145.08	7,044	C 50		C 60	
L	19	50	20°	4½	15° 56' 33"	979.09	L.H.	97.92	88.92	7,044	C 52		C 60	C 53
M	16	40	20°	4½	15° 56' 33"	824.50	R.H.	83.88	74.88	4,920	C 59			C 61
N	34	40	20°	4½	15° 56' 33"	1,752.06	L.H.	168.12	159.12	4,920	C 59	C 58	C59	

* Tooth loadings for max. engine torque of 4,330 lb. in.

§ Rockwell hardness tests of the hub were made at the surface, and at progressive depths below. The results were as follows:—
At surface, C 62; .020" below, C 60; .030" below, C 55; .040" below, C 48; .050" below, C 43.

Table 16

FINAL DRIVE

The general relationship of the final drives will be seen by reference to Fig. 32 and the detail by reference to Figs. 37 and 38, which illustrate the final drive of one of the intermediate axles.

In effect, this final drive is of the double-reduction type, although the relationship of the primary to the secondary reduction is unusual.

Referring to Fig. 32, it will be seen that the lowest or output shaft (B) of the gearbox is extended differential gear (K); each of these bevel-gear sets (FG) is housed in a cast-steel casing attached to the frame.

All final-drive gearboxes are split on a vertical line through the crown-wheel centre-line, and joined by through-bolts and dowels. Per gearbox, there are four bolts of 15 mm. dia. and five of 12 mm. dia.

The final-drive gearbox of each intermediate axle (J) is in three sections, one section serving as a casing

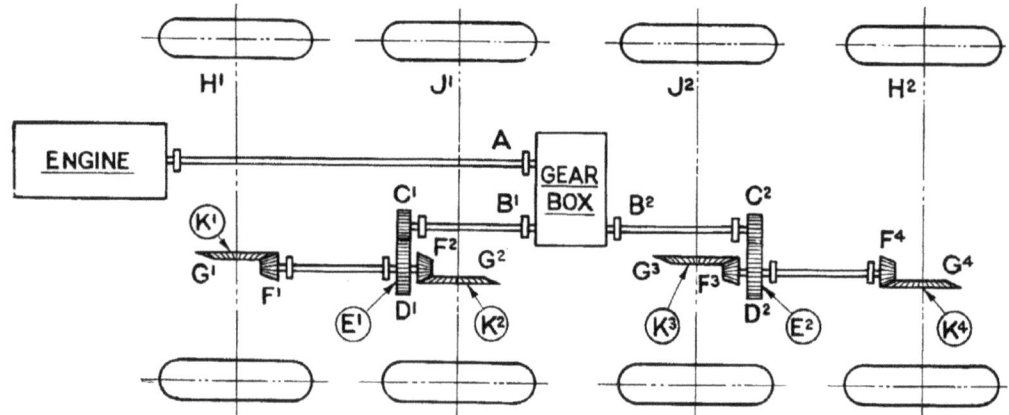

Fig. 32. A diagram showing the lay-out of the transmission system.

fore and aft to convey the drive to two helical-spur reduction gears (CD), one for the front, the other for the rear "bogie."

The spur gears (CD) are used to drop the drive from the level of the gearbox output shaft to the level of the wheel centres.

Each of the two spur-gear sets (CD) is located between, and transmits the drive to, the two axles (H and J) of a bogie, via a differential or compensating gear (E) of the free-wheel type.

Between the road wheels of each axle is a spiral-bevel gear set (FG) incorporating a Z.F. cam-type for the primary reduction gears (CD); the outer final-drive gearboxes enclose bevel gears (FG) only.

Gearing.

Full particulars of the helical-spur and spiral-bevel gears are given in Table 17, together with the tooth loadings.

Bearings.

In general, the bearing mountings of the helical-spur gears (CD) and spiral bevel-gears (FG) are conventional. Screw adjustment is provided for the

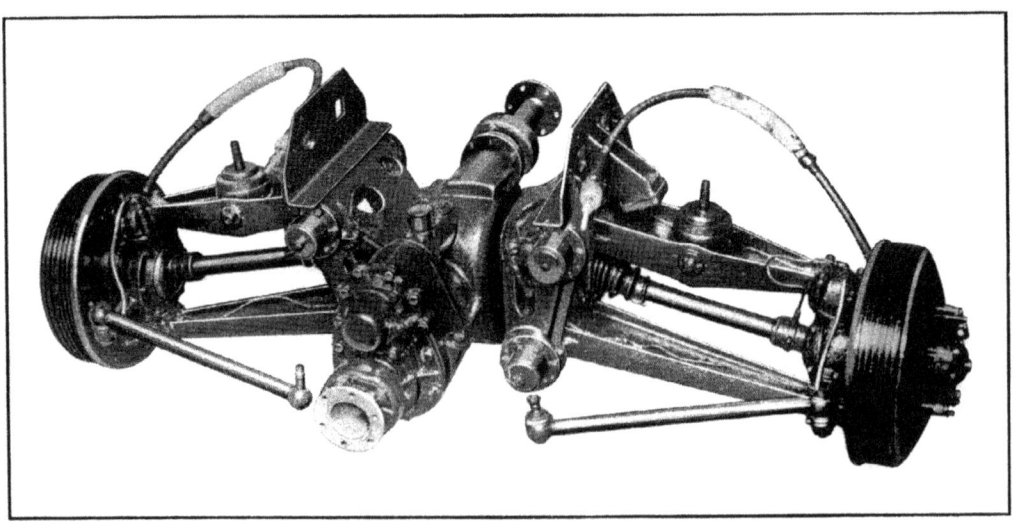

Fig. 33. One of the intermediate axles. The power in-put shaft from the gearbox is at top centre, and the output coupling to front or rear axle at bottom centre.

Fig. 34. The components of the De Lavaud free-wheel. The dogs and slots of the cages are essential features, as explained in the text.

TOOTH LOADING OF FINAL-DRIVE GEARING

Maximum torque, engine	4,332 lb. in.
First speed ratio of main gearbox	10.621 : 1
Maximum torque input to each helical spur pinion	23,005 lb. in.
Number of teeth in helical spur pinion	19
Pitch radius of helical spur pinion teeth	1.752 in.
Face width of helical spur pinion teeth	1.890 in.
Tooth loading, helical gears, per inch face	6,950 lb.
Number of teeth in helical spur wheel	31
Maximum torque input to each bevel pinion	18,767 lb. in.*
Number of teeth in bevel pinion	10
Mean pitch radius of bevel pinion	1.575 in.
Face width of bevel pinion	1.575 in.
Tooth loading, bevels, per inch face	7,560 lb.*
Number of teeth in crown wheel	32
Maximum torque output from each crown wheel	60,054 lb. in.*
Normal laden weight on tyres of one axle	4,410 lb.
Tyre radius, running	17 in.
Maximum torque transmittable by one axle, at 100 per cent. co-efficient of adhesion	75,000 lb. in.

* These values are based on the assumption that the total available torque is shared equally by the four axles, making no allowances for friction losses in the gearing. Adhesion between tyres and ground will prevent these values from being exceeded to any material extent, even when the vehicle is turning. (This condition, in higher gears, would cause all drive to be transmitted to the intermediate axles.)

Table 17

meshing of the crown wheel (G), and shims for that of the bevel pinion (F). As in the other units, however, the readiness of the designers to adopt bearings having inner and outer races of non-standard type is noteworthy.

Inter-axle Differential.

On full lock, the front and rear wheels describe circles having a mean radius of 17.4 ft., whereas the intermediate work on a mean radius of 15.8 ft.

In one full circle at full lock, therefore, the front and rear crown-wheels (G1 and G4) complete 12.275 revolutions, the intermediate crown-wheels (G2 and G3) 11.12 revolutions.

A De Lavaud compensating gear (E) is housed in each of the primary reduction sets (CD) of the final drive, to provide the necessary differential action, and thereby avoid inter-axle fight, and consequent power loss.

Each compensating gear (E) comprises two interlocked roller-type free-wheels, both housed inside and driven by the output wheel (D) of the primary reduction gearing, and each driving one of the bevel pinions (F). Details of the compensating gear (E) are shown in Fig. 34.

Each row of free-wheel rollers is contained by a separate cage and the two adjacent cages are provided with male and female spring-loaded plungers, which engage with each other and have the effect of producing a slight torque tending to align the rollers of one cage with those of the other. These plungers are seen in Fig. 34.

One of the cages is provided at one end with dogs projecting into slots in the adjacent end of the other cage.

Fig. 36 is intended to make clear the principle of operation of the free-wheels and also shows the function of the dogs and slots (D and S) in the roller cages.

Referring to Fig. 34, it will be noted that the roller-jamming cams take the form of shallow cylindrical recesses cut into the bore of the spur wheel, and that the wedge-action can take place in either direction of rotation. The inner, or driven, members are plain cylindrical hubs, internally splined.

The left-hand view of Fig. 36 shows the condition with both free-wheels jammed, i.e. driving. In this

Fig. 35. Details of the Z.F. differential; signs of wear are evident in the outer and inner members as well as on the plungers.

condition, the rollers of one cage are aligned with the rollers of the other by the spring-loaded plungers mentioned above, and dogs (D) are centrally disposed in slots (S).

Under the pressure of the plunger springs, friction clutch facings (lying between flanges on the roller cages and the driven hubs of the free-wheels) induce drag, which tends to revolve the cages with their corresponding driven hubs.

The provision of the free-wheels for the intermediate axles is necessary to enable the outer axles to revolve faster than the inner axles in either direction of running; it would, of course, also allow the intermediate axles to revolve faster than outer axles.

The action of this free-wheel compensating gear is unlike that of an ordinary bevel differential. It cannot equalise the drive; in fact, all drive is transmitted to the intermediate axles when the vehicle is turning. On the other hand, if an axle loses adhesion, the others continue to drive.

According to the manufacturers' statement, a De Lavaud differential of the size employed should be capable of transmitting, for short periods only, a torque of 2,745 lb. ft.

Inter-wheel Differential

A differential gear of the cam-type developed by Zahnradfabrik Friedrichshafen, is provided in each of the final drives, to sub-divide the drive between wheels on opposite sides of the vehicle.

In their brochure, dealing with this device, the makers described it as " a self-locking differential " and claimed that it possessed a high resistance to wheel-spin. This property was stated to be due to the considerable internal friction of the differential, arising out of the high intensity of pressure on the cam surfaces. A diagram in this brochure gave a

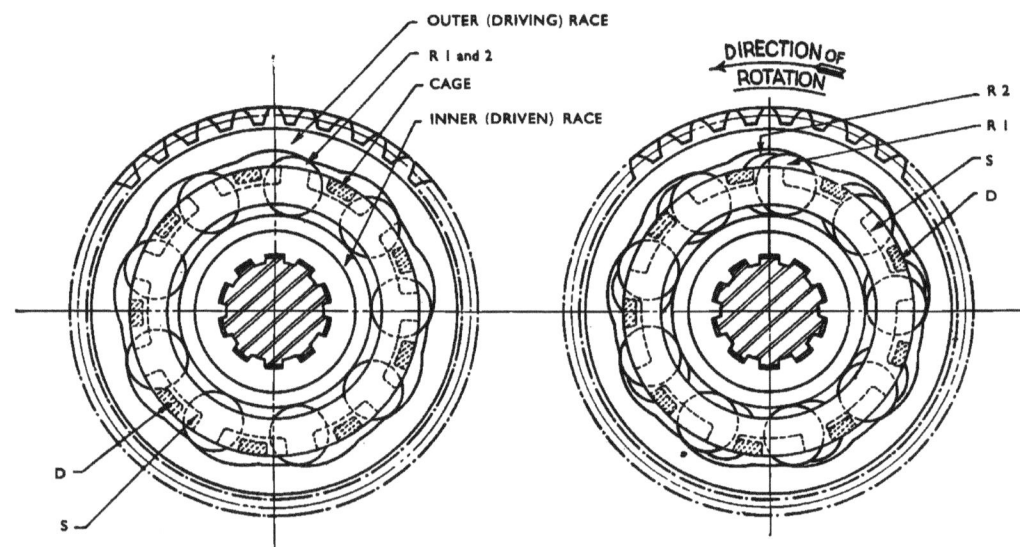

Fig. 36. This diagram shows two conditions of drive in the De Lavaud free-wheel.

The right-hand view of Fig. 36 shows the position of the cages and rollers when the vehicle is turning; under these conditions, rollers (R1), which are associated with the slower-moving inner axle, are transmitting the drive, and are also holding the dogs (D) of their cage in a fixed position in relation to the cam profiles. On the other hand, the faster moving outer axle has, through the friction of the clutch-facings, caused its associated cage to move ahead of the other cage, to the extent of the play permitted by slots (S), and this has not only allowed the rollers (R2) to become free, but has also prevented them from coming into contact with the opposite flanks of the cams.

maximum efficiency of only 44 per cent. for the Z.F. differential, as compared with 85 per cent. for a normal bevel-gear unit.

The relationship of this differential to the final-drive gearing is shown in Figs. 32, 37 and 38, and its construction is illustrated in Fig. 35.

It will be seen that the driven members A and B are, essentially, two cylindrical hubs of different diameters, arranged concentrically (when assembled) and each splined to one of the axle-shafts; cam lobes are formed on the outside of A and on the inside of B.

Between these inner and outer cams is a single row of plungers, C, rectangular in section, designed

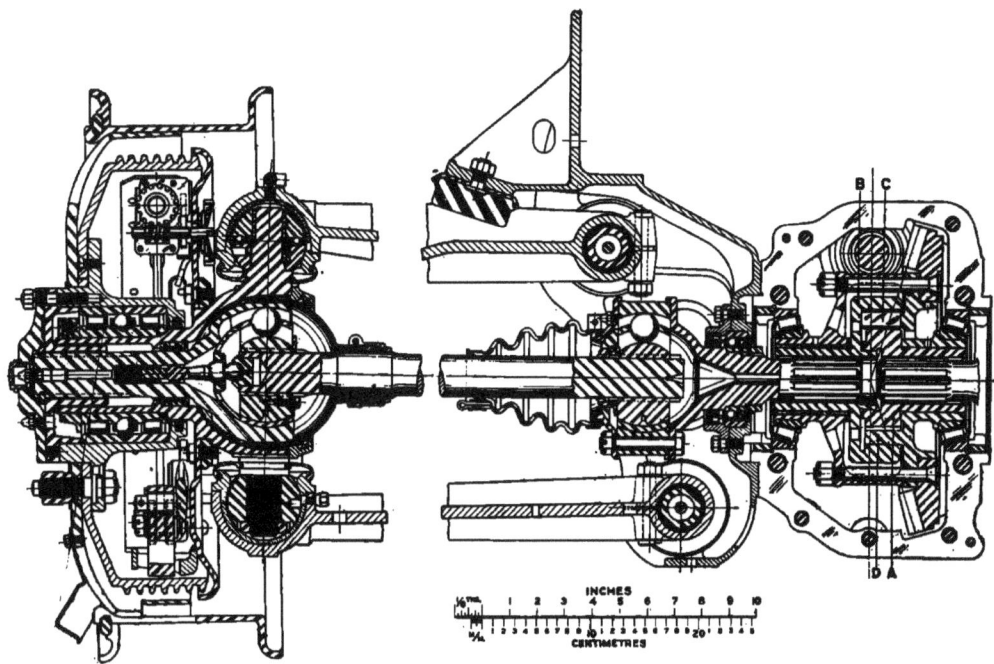

Fig. 37. The final drive—a section through hub, universal-joints and differential gear.

to slide radially in slots formed in the cage D, which is attached to the crown wheel, and forms the driving member.

The rounded outer and inner ends of plungers C project from cage D, and are at all times in contact with the cam surfaces of A and B respectively. The radial space between the outer and inner cam rings is such that the plungers can traverse the cam surface only when the crests of one member coincide with the troughs in the other.

In straight-ahead driving, the plungers are forced between the opposing slopes of the cams, and the opposing forces thereby created are so nearly equal that the plungers do not slide in their slots, and consequently both driven members are carried round at the same speed as the driving member. Differential action does not occur until the conditions promoting it are sufficiently powerful to overcome the internal resistance of the unit.

When both road wheels of an axle are jacked up and the crown wheel is held against rotation, if one wheel is revolved, the other turns in the opposite direction. In this respect, the Z.F. differential functions in the same way as the normal type, but whereas in the conventional unit both sides turn at the same speed in the Z.F. unit one side revolves faster than the other, in the ratio of 13 to 11.

This curious feature arises from the fact that, if the member A is turned through one revolution while the cage D is held, each plunger C is caused to move in and out 11 times by the 11 lobes of A; each plunger oscillation causes a translation of one cam-lobe of member B, but as B has 13 lobes, 11 oscillations cause it to revolve 11/13 of a turn.

The torque transmitted to member B therefore exceeds that transmitted to member A, in the ratio of 13 : 11, i.e. by 18 per cent.

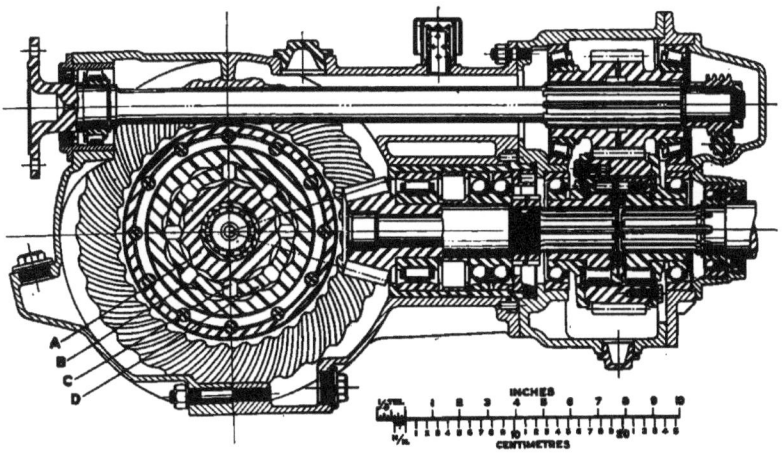

Fig. 38. A sectional view of the final-drive casing, showing, on the left, the Z.F. differential, and, on the right, the De Lavaud free-wheel.

The differentials used in the Bussing-NAG armoured car are Z.F. size 11a, which is rated by the makers as having a maximum capacity of 3,000 lb. ft.; however, in this vehicle the differential can be subjected to a torque of over 5,000 lb. ft., as shown in Table 17.

Under these conditions, the plungers are forced against the cams with great pressure, the intensity of loading being in the order of 10 tons per inch of linear contact.

In this differential, high pressure-loading is accompanied by sliding, and it is not surprising that the plungers of the two units which were stripped showed signs of scuffing and incipient seizure on the cam-engagement surfaces.

Constant-velocity Joints

The eight road wheels of this vehicle are coupled to the final-drive gearboxes by means of eight exposed axle-shafts, each of which is fitted with two Rzeppa constant-velocity joints. All details of these joints appear to conform with the detail description given in the makers' catalogue.

The inner joint is a 1½-in. disc-type "symbol E" joint which is rated by the makers to work at a maximum angle of 15°. It is worth noting that the location of the articulation straps is such as to permit these joints to work at an angle of approximately 19° which might account for the fact that in one or two cases the shafts had broken.

The outer joint is a 1¼-in. bell-type "symbol E" joint, having a rated working angle of 37°. In the Bussing-NAG vehicle, this joint attains a maximum angle of 30°, the resultant of steering and articulation.

Both joints are rated by the makers to transmit 17,800 lb.-in., subject to a temporary overload of 50 per cent., but assuming that the drive is equally divided over the eight shafts, the total torque derived from the engine and the lowest gear ratio is 30,027 lb.-in. per joint.

Nevertheless, when stripped, these joints were found to be in good condition, the wearing surfaces being marked, but not indented to any measurable extent.

HUBS AND STUB AXLES

The hubs and stub axles are of very light design and incorporate bearings of an unusual type, in which the single inner sleeve has tracks for two roller races and also for a single row of balls. The detail construction of the hubs and their bearings is illustrated in Fig. 37.

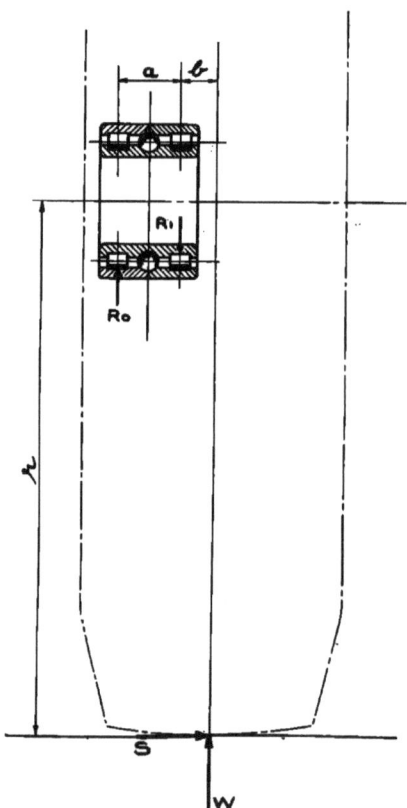

Fig. 39. This sketch (to scale) shows the narrow spacing of the hub bearings and their considerable offset from the wheel-centre.

Hub and Stub Axle Loading
(See Fig. 39)

Symbols

W	Weight of vehicle per wheel	2,205 lb.
r	Running radius of tyre	17 in.
	Bending moment due to cornering	37,500 in. lb.
	Outside dia. of stub axle at root	2.756 in.
	Inside dia. of stub axle at root	2.362 in.
	Section Modulus of stub axle at root	.946 in.³
	Bending Stress in stub axle at root	17.7 tons/in.²
$\dfrac{b+a}{a}$	Leverage—weight on wheel acting on inner radial bearing	1.6 : 1
	Reaction on inner bearing due to static weight	3,525 lb.
$\dfrac{b}{a}$	Leverage—weight on wheel acting on outer radial bearing	.6 : 1
	Reaction on outer bearing due to static weight	1,320 lb.
$\dfrac{r}{a}$	Ratio—running radius of tyre to centres of radial bearing	8.64 : 1
	Reaction on each radial bearing due to cornering	19,030 lb.
R_1	Resultant reaction on inner radial bearing	22,555 lb.
R_0	Resultant reaction on outer radial bearing	20,350 lb.

The condition referred to above as "cornering" assumes a load "S" (equal to the static weight per wheel) acting on the tyre at the ground in a direction towards the centre of the vehicle.

Table 18

The unusually narrow spacing of the roller races is noteworthy and cannot be considered as a good feature of the hub layout. The resultant high loading of the roller bearings has been further aggravated by locating both bearings well outside the line of vertical loading through the tyre centre.

When the A.C.V. chassis was being re-conditioned to enable performance trials to be carried out, it was found necessary to change several of the hub assemblies, due to play which had developed in these hub bearings. Particulars of these bearings and their loadings are given in Table 18.

The stub axle appears to be unusually frail inside the hub bearings, but the proportions are, nevertheless, not such as to give a particularly low factor of safety. An estimate of the stress in the stub axle when cornering is also included in Table 18.

Unorthodox features of the hub layout are the use of a felt seal, and the omission of the usual dowelled portion of the hub-flange driving studs.

WHEELS AND TYRES

Wheels.

The wheels are of conventional pressed-steel disc three-piece type. The major particulars of these wheels are as follows :—

Rim base dia.		18 in.
Distance between rim flanges inside	123	mm.
Height of fixed rim flanges above base	35	mm.
Height of detachable rim flanges above base	30	mm.
Offset to outside of wheel disc	110	mm.
Thickness of wheel-stud flange	10.5	mm.
No. of wheel studs		6
Dia. of wheel studs	18	mm.
Pitch circle dia. of studs	205	mm.
Form of wheel-nut seating		Spherical
Pitch of wheel-nut thread	2 mm. (all threads R.H.)	
Weight of complete wheel		67.5 lb.
Location of brake-drum	Outside hub flange	

Tyres.

All tyres are of the 210 mm. × 18 in. size and are of the low-pressure cord-reinforced type.

The majority of the tyres on both vehicles are of Continental " Extra-Gelande " manufacture ; some of these have natural rubber treads and walls with durometer hardness value of 58 ; others appear to be made of synthetic rubber, presumably " Buna " and have a durometer hardness value of 62.

One of the tyres was of the " Dekagrip " type, and appears to be made of synthetic rubber.

The inner tubes of the Continental tyres are unusual in having a thick internal coating of red plastic rubber, apparently intended to be self-sealing.

On level ground, and with full load, the weight imposed on each tyre is approximately 1 ton.

When crossing trenches, it is possible that the load on any one tyre will be raised to 2 tons.

The maker's rating for this size of tyre is not known, but the Michelin Company rate their commercial pattern at 1.275 tons.

SUSPENSION

Each of the eight road wheels is linked to the frame by two swinging levers, one above and the other below, the shaft coupling the road wheel to its final-drive gearbox.

The inner end of each of these levers is splined and secured by two pinch-bolts to a short longitudinal shaft carried in two widely spaced rubber-bushed nesses of the various sections are approximately the same for upper and lower levers, although the duties performed are very different, in that the upper lever alone carries the very considerable bending moment due to the upward reaction of the wheel.

The upward movement of the wheels is limited by rubber pads attached to suitable extensions of the

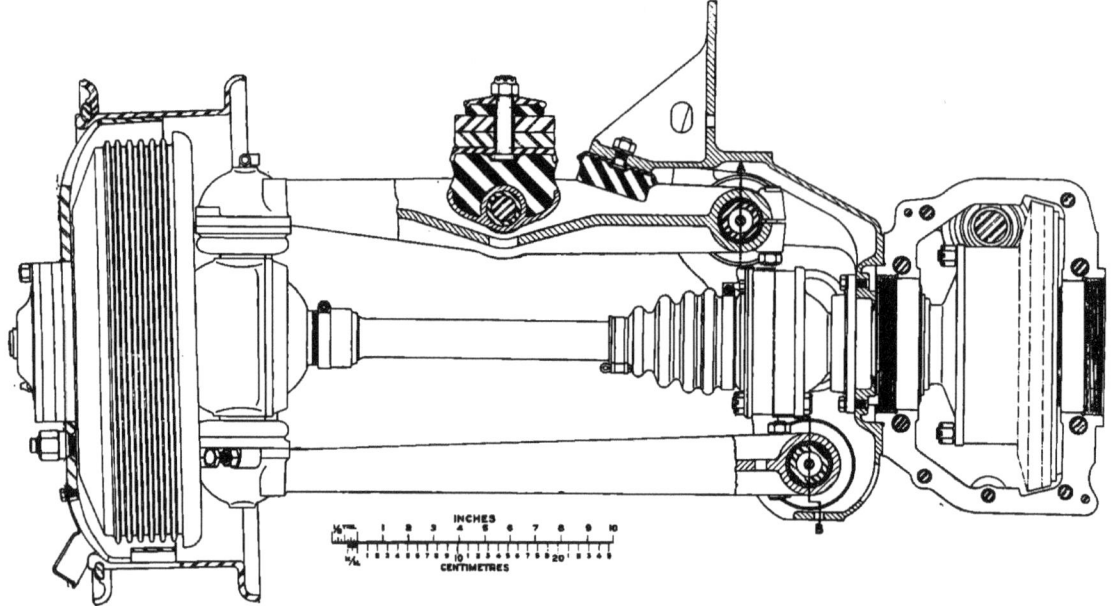

Fig. 40. A general arrangement of a pair of suspension links, showing their attachment to frame, spring and stub axle.

bearings. These are attached to the brackets which secure the final-drive gearboxes to the frame.

At their outer ends, the levers are provided with spherical sockets engaging spherical bearings on the stub axle, one above, the other below, the wheel centre-line. These ball joints allow for the rise and fall of the wheel, and are also the equivalent to the normal king pin of the steering knuckle.

The construction of the suspension links is shown in Figs. 37, 40, 42 and 44. Figs. 41 and 43 show one of the four leaf-type suspension springs, which are mounted outside and parallel to the frame side-members; each spring is pivoted to an extension of a cross tube of the frame and the spring-ends bear on the upper suspension levers through the intermediary of rubber blocks, one to each lever.

These rubber blocks are bonded to cast-steel brackets which are pivotally attached to the suspension levers so that they can remain horizontal whatever the inclination of the suspension levers; their distortion also accommodates the lateral and transverse movement of the springs relative to the levers, which would entail an awkward construction in metal. A bolt, passing through a slotted hole in each spring-end, keeps the latter in contact with its rubber-block assembly.

The lower suspension levers are longer than the upper levers, and the disposition of the pivots has been well selected to cause relatively small variation in the inclination of the wheels and steering knuckles, due to their rise and fall. This point is illustrated in Fig. 45.

Both upper and lower suspension levers are of I-section, with the flanges vertical, and the thick-

final-drive suspension brackets. These are illustrated in Fig. 44.

The downward movement of the wheels is limited by check-straps of flat plaited steel wire. These straps have an eye at each end, engaging pins on the upper suspension link and on the hull, respectively. These straps appear to be highly stressed, as out of 16 on two vehicles, only one was still serviceable, the remainder having been replaced in the field by temporary straps of ordinary steel cable.

There appears to be a need for the incorporation of some form of buffer in these suspension straps to relieve the shocks which they have to take when crossing trenches, etc.

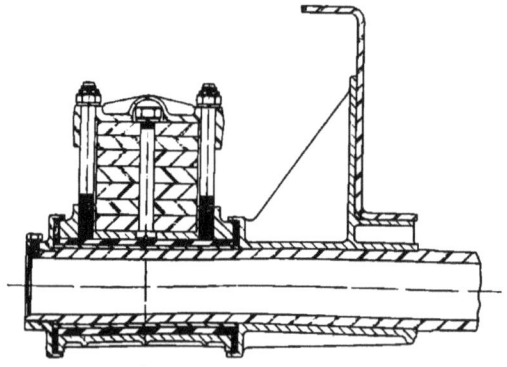

Fig. 41. The tubular frame cross-member is extended to form the pivot for the rocking spring-anchorage which is provided with a rubber bush.

The total articulation movement, and the effect of this on the wheel and steering-knuckle inclination, is shown in Fig. 45.

The shafts carrying the inner ends of the suspension levers are splined into the inner bushes of their Silentbloc-type rubber bearings, as shown in Figs. 42 and 44. Dimensional and loading particulars of these bushes are shown in Table 21.

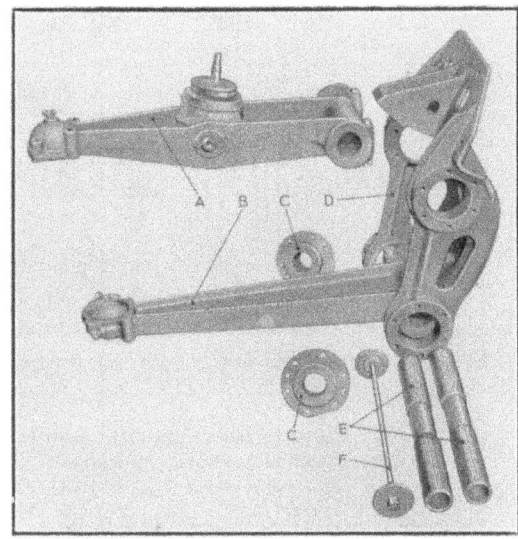

Fig. 44 Suspension-link details. A. Upper link. B. Lower link. C. Rubber bush in housing. D. Frame bracket, supporting also final-drive gearbox. E. Splined pivot-shafts. F. Tie-bar for cover-plates.

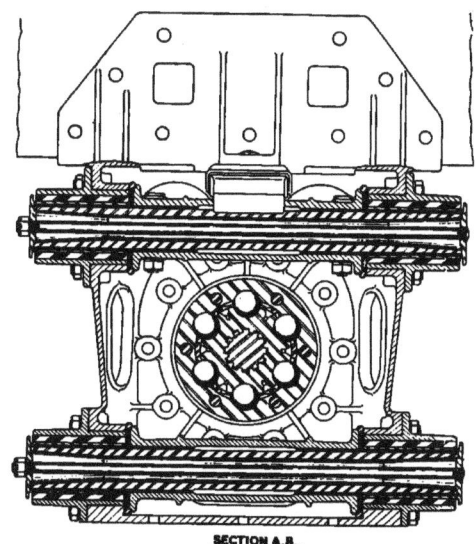

Fig. 42. A section of the suspension-link pivots through line AB, Fig. 40.

Particulars of the leaf springs, which are conventional in detail design, are given in Table 22.

The deflection of the springs from free to full load is only 2.27 in. but, due to the multiplying effect of the suspension levers, the corresponding deflection measured at the wheel is 4.77 in.

An interesting feature of this spring is the construction of the central pivot, which comprises a rubber bearing of the Silentbloc type. The inner bush of this bearing is a sliding fit on the extended end of the bogie cross-tube, and is clamped against rotation only by the end-pressure of a large nut.

These bearings all showed signs of distress, the rubber having become displaced from the lower to the upper side of the bearing in each case, the eccentricity amounting to .059 in. There was also evidence of the rubber bond fracturing at the top.

Dimensions and loadings of this bush are also given in Table 21.

Suspension-System Weights	lb.
Upper suspension arm, complete with rubber-block assembly	34
Lower suspension arm	22
Leaf spring assembly, complete with centre-pivot bracket, bolts, etc.	208

Table 19

Unsprung Weights	lb.
Hub assembly and part of shaft	155
Wheel ..	67.5
Tyre	77
Tube	3.5
Unsprung part of top arm	15.5
Unsprung part of lower arm ..	8.5
Total unsprung weight, per wheel ..	327.0
Total unsprung weight of vehicle	2,616.0
Ratio, sprung to unsprung weight	5.743 : 1

Table 20

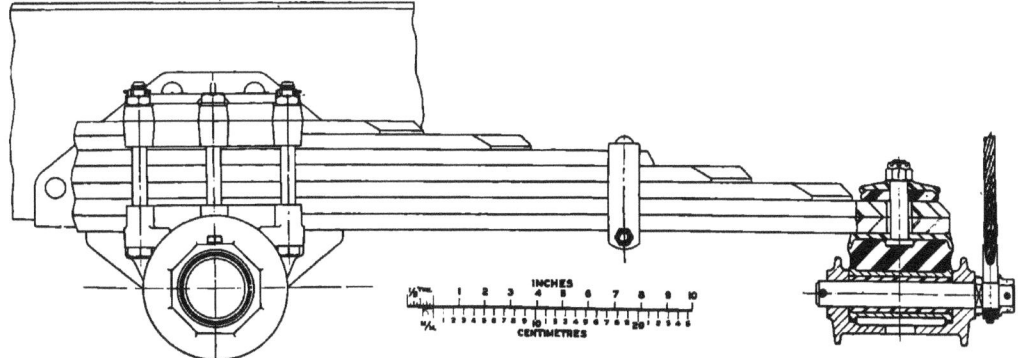

Fig. 43. Part of a main spring. The pivot pin below the rubber attachment to the upper suspension link (see also Fig. 40) has no provision for lubrication and, in some cases, had seized.

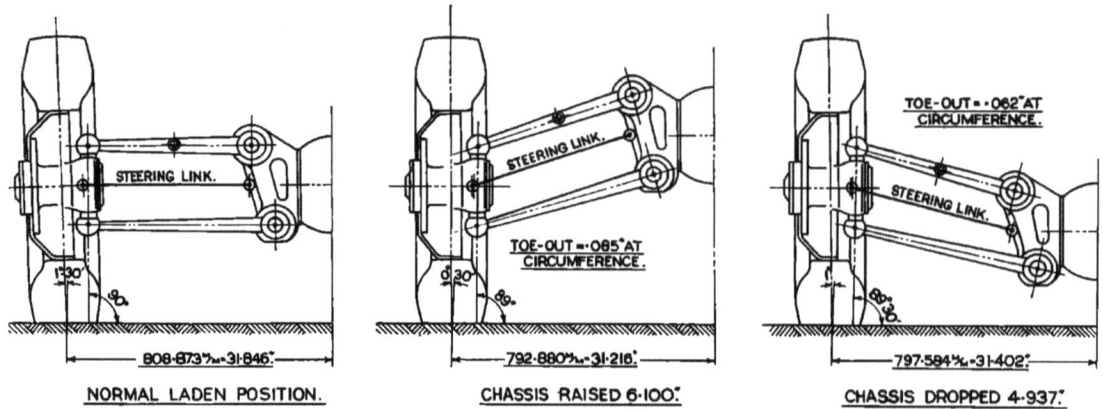

Fig. 45. The angular and lateral movement of a stub-axle through the range of articulation between frame stop-limits. Variation of toe-out is set up by interference between the suspension links and the steering link during articulation.

LOADING OF RUBBER BEARINGS IN SUSPENSION SYSTEM

Symbol (See Fig. 46)

	Total weight of vehicle	17,640 lb.
	Total unsprung weight	2,616 lb.
	Total sprung weight	15,024 lb.
W	Sprung weight, per wheel	1,878 lb.
b/a	Ratio of suspension link lengths	2.108 : 1
R_1	Vertical reaction at spring end	3,960 lb.
R_2	Vertical reaction at bearing "B"	2,082 lb.
d/c	Ratio of tyre offset to knuckle centres	.331 : 1
R_3	Horizontal force along suspension link	622 lb.
	Resultant force on bearing "B"	2,176 lb.
	Inside dia. of bearing "B"	1.97 in.
	Aggregate length of bearing "B"	7.40 in.
	Total projected area of bearing "B"	14.58 sq. in.
	Loading per sq. in of bearing "B"	149 lb.
R_4	Vertical reaction at bearing "A"	7,920 lb.
	Inside dia. of bearing "A"	3.15 in.
	Length of bearing "A"	6.69 in.
	Projected area of bearing "A"	21.07 sq. in.
	Loading per sq. in. of bearing "A"	376 lb.

NOTE.

In the above table, the values given for bearing loads are those due to static weight only; these, being constant in direction, play the chief part in determining the proportions of rubber bearings.

Loads additional to those given, are produced, in bearings "B" and "C," by cornering, braking and driving forces, the resultant bearing loads being subject to wide variations in magnitude and direction.

Table 21

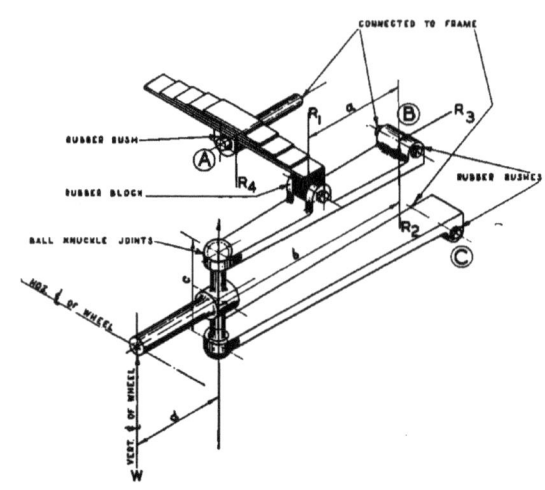

Fig. 46. An orthographic diagram of one unit of the suspension system. For references, see the accompanying Table 21.

LEAF SPRING DATA

Symbol (See Note)

	Number of plates	7
t	Plate thickness (5 plates)	0.630 in.
	(2 plates)	0.551 in.
	Plate width	3.937 in.
	Normal static load on each spring	7,920 lb.
L	Spring-eye centres	54.331 in.
d	Corresponding spring deflection	2.273 in.
f	Plate stress in main leaf at normal static load, tons per sq. in.	25.0

NOTE.

Plate stress is derived from the formula :—

$$f = \frac{52{,}800 \, d.t.}{L^2}$$

Table 22

STEERING GEAR

The steering system of this vehicle is extremely complicated owing to the provision of a steering wheel and column at each end of the chassis, to enable the vehicle to be conveniently driven at speed in either direction. This system has necessitated coupling the two steering wheels together by 10 small bevel gears, and a shaft running lengthwise along the shaft is 1 : 1, but the top of the front steering column is provided with two special bevel gears enabling the steering-wheel spindle to be set at an angle of 80° to the column. A curious feature of the design is that the bevel wheel on the hand-wheel spindle has

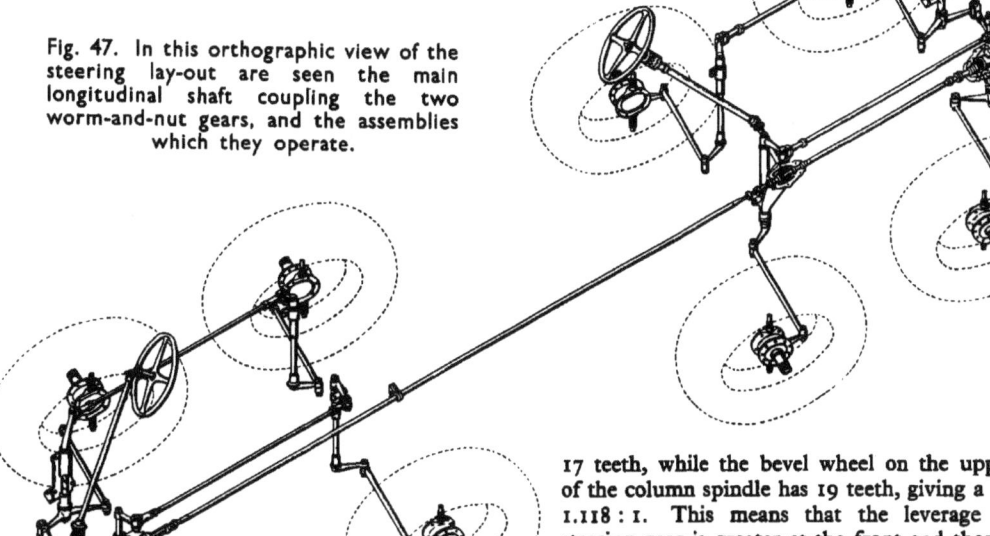

Fig. 47. In this orthographic view of the steering lay-out are seen the main longitudinal shaft coupling the two worm-and-nut gears, and the assemblies which they operate.

17 teeth, while the bevel wheel on the upper end of the column spindle has 19 teeth, giving a ratio of 1.118 : 1. This means that the leverage of the steering gear is greater at the front end than at the rear end of the vehicle.

The bevel gearing at the top of the front steering column has been adopted to give the maximum convenience to the driver in the rather limited space available. The upper portion of the wheel rim is closer to the driver's body than the lower portion, i.e. the opposite to the usual arrangement.

The rear steering wheel has a dog-clutch which is automatically disengaged by the forward-and-reverse pedals when the vehicle is travelling forwards. This wheel is mounted normally, i.e. with its spindle concentric with the steering column.

left-hand side of the vehicle (looking forward from the front driver's seat).

The ratio of all bevel gears coupling the two steering column spindles with this long horizontal

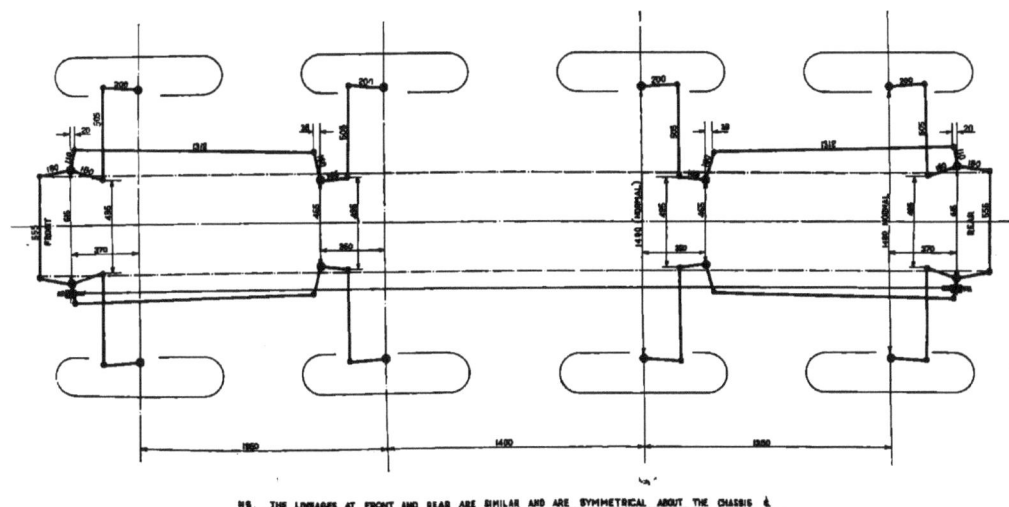

Fig. 48. A diagram (to scale) of the steering connections, showing the lengths of rods and levers.

Page Thirty-seven

The ends of the longitudinal steering shaft are coupled to the worm shafts of two worm-and-nut type steering gearboxes, each of which operates a vertical shaft linked by a system of rods and levers to the four stub axles of a bogie. The sole connection, therefore, between the steering system of the front bogie and that of the rear bogie is the longitudinal shaft.

articulation of the suspension links to a slight extent as shown below :—
(a) Wheels raised to limit of articulation stops .. 0° 30' (in at top)
(b) Axle shaft, horizontal .. 0° (vertical)
(c) Wheels dropped to limit of articulation stops .. .. 1° (in at top)

It would appear that the above slight inclinations

Fig. 49. The steering linkage for one pair of wheels is clearly seen in this front-end view of the chassis.

It will be noted that there are 12 pin-and-jaw type connections and 16 ball-and-socket joints, making a total of 28 joints in the rod system. The detail construction of the bevel gears, worm-and-nut gears and of the horizontal steering shaft, is shown in Fig. 50.

Four small universal joints of interesting design are used in the horizontal shaft and are also employed in the change-speed controls. A detail of these joints also appears in Fig. 50.

Steering Geometry.

The lengths and angles of the various levers of the steering system (see Fig. 48) have been carefully selected, and investigation has shown that, under all conditions of lock, the axes of all stub axles intersect at a common centre on a line midway between the bogie centres. The various angles of the stub axles on full lock are :—

	Inside	Outside
Front and rear wheels ..	26°	19¼°
Intermediate wheels	16¼°	12¼°

As the vehicle has been designed to steer equally well in either direction, the steering pivots are vertical in side elevation. They are also substantially vertical when viewed from the end of the vehicle, and, in consequence, the wheels have little or no tendency to return to the straight-ahead position.

The outward rake of the steering-knuckle axis, relative to the vertical, varies in accordance with the

could have been increased with advantage to the general stability of the steering.

The following measurements of the toe-in and toe-out were made at the wheel rims :—
Front axle .. .. 1/16 in. toe-in
Front intermediate axle ⅛ in. toe-out
Rear intermediate axle 1/16 in. toe-out
Rear axle .. .. .. 1/16 in. toe-out

As the vehicle is intended to operate in either direction at full speed, it would be difficult to operate with any large degree of toe-in or toe-out setting.

The following are measurements of wheel-camber relative to the vertical :—

Wheel-Camber		
	L.H. Side	R.H. Side
Front axle	1°	0° 54'
Front intermediate axle	1° 58'	1° 26'
Rear intermediate axle	1° 48'	1° 15'
Rear axle	1° 48'	1° 4'

Table 23

These camber measurements were taken with the vehicle standing on level ground, and fully laden.

It is our opinion that the variations in the toe-out and toe-in settings, and in the wheel cambers, are incidental and have no particular significance.

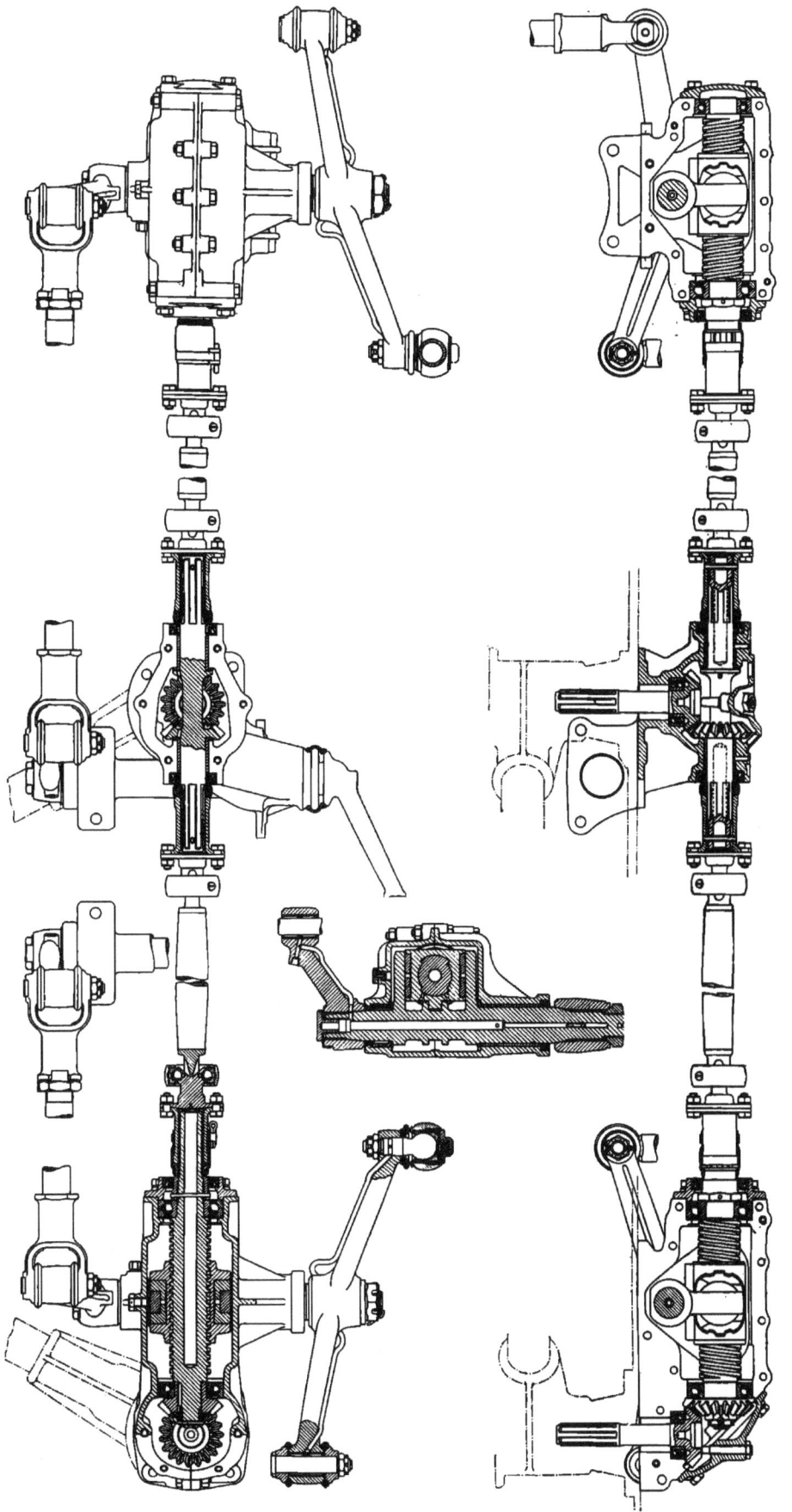

Fig. 50. The upper view shows the longitudinal shaft-line in elevation, partly sectioned; in the centre is a vertical section of the worm-and-nut gear, through the axis of the rocking shaft. At the foot is a plan view (partly in section) of the above units.

Constructional Particulars.

1. *Gearing at top of Front Steering Column.*
   (a) *Driving Pinion on Hand Wheel Shaft—Straight teeth.*
   - Number of teeth .. 17
   - Pitch dia. 45.5 mm.
   - Face width 18 mm.

   (b) *Driven Gear.*
   - Number of teeth .. 19
   - Pitch dia. 66.5 mm.
   - Pitch module 3.5 mm.
   - Face width 18 mm.

2. *All other Bevel Gears—Straight teeth.*
   - Number of teeth .. 19
   - Pitch dia. 66.5 mm.
   - Pitch module 3.5 mm.
   - Face width (approx.) 16 mm.

3. *Worm-and-Nut Gears.*
   - Number of starts 2
   - Top dia. of Thread (nominal) 45 mm.
   - Bottom dia. of thread 37 mm.
   - Axial pitch of thread (advance) 16 mm.
   - Form of thread Square
   - Threaded length of nut 90 mm.
   - Material of worm Steel
   - Material of nut Phosphor bronze

Ratio—Output shaft to input shaft torque.
   (a) In mid position 21.6 : 1
   (b) In end position 30 : 1

4. *Horizontal Steering Shaft.*
	Front	Rear
Outside dia. of tube	35 mm.	30 mm.
Inside dia. of tube	28 mm.	23 mm.

5. *Rod Linkage.*
   - Pin-and-jaw bearings dia. 23 mm. O.D. × 18 mm. I.D. (needle rollers)
   - Ball-and-socket joints, type Spring-loaded cup
   - Ball pillars Tapered shank
   - Ball dia. .. 30 mm.
   - Ball pillars, top dia. of cone .. 20 mm.
   - Ball pillars, included angle of cone 1 in 10 = 5° 42'

6. *Handwheels*
   - Dia. 495 mm.

BRAKING SYSTEM

Each wheel is provided with a two-shoe full-wrap brake of Bendix Servo pattern, generally similar in type to that used for track brakes in the German tank, type PZKWIII, but having woven asbestos linings instead of cast-iron facings. This type of brake appears to possess a very high shoe factor, or degree of self-energisation (ratio approximately 5 : 1); consequently, quite a good brake performance is obtainable, although the vehicle is not fitted with a booster. In this connection, the high overall leverage adopted for both hand and foot systems no doubt plays a part. The construction of the brake is shown in Fig. 51.

When the shoes are expanded, by the wedge moving against the shoe-tip rollers, the leading shoe reacts against the trailing shoe via the floating adjuster assembly, thereby forcing the trailing end of the trailing shoe into contact with an abutment-

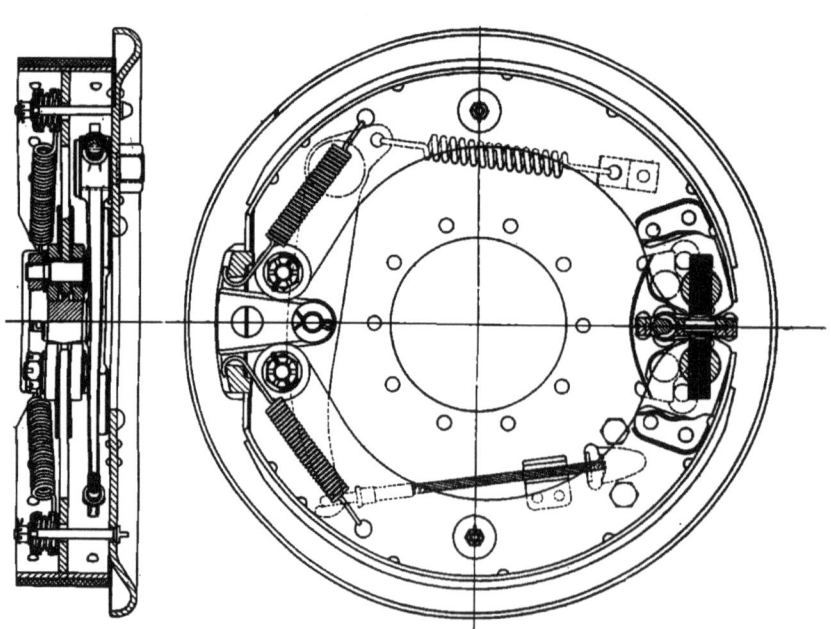

Fig. 51. Section and end-elevation of a brake assembly, showing details of the cable-operated wedge-expander and adjuster.

piece surrounding the wedge. The adjuster unit is returned to the central position after the brake application by the centralising action of two small bell-crank levers, acted upon by a spring of curved strip steel.

The adjuster mechanism, seen in Figs. 37 and 51, is of ingenious construction and gives an unusually fine adjustment. It comprises a small worm drive in which a worm wheel is provided with a threaded extension spindle, each end engaging a threaded trunnion in the adjacent end of the brake-shoe. These trunnions are tapped with right and left-hand threads, so that rotation of the worm wheel alters the distance between the trunnions. The wormshaft is extended through a slotted hole in the brake back-plate and carries a hand-wheel for the brake adjustment. The worm has a single thread and the wheel has 15 teeth. The threads in the trunnions have a pitch of 1 mm. One turn of the adjuster therefore causes a movement at each shoe-centre of .0013 in.

The brake-linkage between the expander wedges and the operating pedals and levers comprises the following elements :—

(1) Eight wedge-operating levers, each pivoted to one of the brake back-plates, as shown in Fig. 51.
(2) Eight flexible cables linking the wedge-operating levers to relay-levers on the chassis frame.
(3) A system of cross-shafts and rods linking the relay-levers to the pedals and hand brake levers.

By the provision of slotted links for lost motion, the same rods serve for both hand- and foot-systems.

Dimensions, etc.

Brake drum, inside dia.	14.76 in.
Brake-shoe width	2.56 in.
Brake-drum, total area	950 sq. in.
Brake lining, total area	733 sq. in.
Ratio, vehicle weight to drum area	17 lb./sq. in.
Ratio, vehicle weight to lining area	24 lb./sq. in.
Ratio, drum radius to tyre radius	.446 : 1
Ratio, pedal-plate travel to shoe-centre travel	184 : 1
Ratio, hand-grip travel to shoe-centre travel	354 : 1

The following gives the maximum travel of the principal parts :—

Pedal	6.25 in.
Rod from pedal to cross-shaft	1.51 in.*
Cable	1.15 in.*
Expander wedge	.538 in.*
Shoe tip	.068 in.*
Shoe centre	.034 in.*

* Calculated from movement of pedal-pad, which is the limiting factor, no allowance having been made for stretch or clearances at bearings.

RADIATOR

This unit comprises two sections, the main section being for water-cooling the engine, the auxiliary for cooling the engine lubricating oil. The whole unit is carried on rubber pads bearing directly on the top flanges of the frame side-members and is located between the engine and the main compartment of the hull.

The air is admitted to the radiator through hand-adjustable louvres in the hull top-plate, and guided to the forward side of the radiator by a system of inclined baffle plates. Before passing through the main or water-cooling system, the air traverses a single row of gilled tubes mounted on the forward side of the main stack. The air is drawn through the radiator by two cast-aluminium fans, located on the rear side of the unit. These fans revolve in bearings supported by arms cast integrally with the aluminium alloy fan-shrouds. Outlet air from the

Fig. 52. The mountings for the twin fans are carried by arms cast integral with the cowling, and attached to the radiator.

Fig. 53. The oil-cooler side of the radiator, showing also (at bottom right) the semi-rotary type oil-filter which is connected to the accelerator pedal.

fans is blown past the engine and ejected from the vehicle through louvres in the hinged rear plate of the engine housing. Adjustable shutters are provided in the bulkhead between the driving compartment and the radiators to allow a proportion of the input air to be drawn from the fighting compartment, if desired, for ventilation. Each fan is driven by a "V" belt by a two-grooved pulley extension from the engine-shaft driving the water pump and dynamo.

The main radiator is of the integral, or dipped-core, type, the film-type cooling stack being soldered directly to sheet-metal tanks and side standards. The side standards are unusual in that they incorporate water passages, conveying water from the two cylinder-head connections to the top tank. The radiator is vented to atmosphere in the normal way.

The oil-cooling element is simply a single length of 10 mm. outside dia. tubing, wound to and fro across the radiator 10 times, in order to provide the necessary cooling surface in conjunction with vertical fins, while maintaining at the same time a reasonably high oil-flow velocity to avoid stagnation. This construction is illustrated by Fig. 53, which also shows the main features of the water-cooling radiator. Details of the fans and their mountings are shown in Fig. 52.

Oil Radiator

Type	Gilled tube
Tubes, No. of	10
Outside dia.	10 mm.
Length	755 mm.
No. of gills	121
Width of gills	20 mm.
Length of gills	275 mm.
Frontal area	2,076 sq. cm. (2.24 sq. ft.)
Total cooling surface	15 sq. ft.
Weight of complete radiator (dry)	14 lb.

Water Radiator

Radiator, type	Film
Width	915 mm.
Height	430 mm.
Thickness	110 mm.
Frontal area	3,934 sq. cm. (4.24 sq. ft.)

Fans

No.	2
Speed	1.15 engine speed
Dia.	460 mm.
No. of blades	8
Weight of complete water radiator (dry)	125 lb.

FUEL SYSTEM

The main fuel tank is of rectangular shape and mounted between the frame side-members in front of the gearbox.

Due to space considerations, it has a capacity of only 24 gallons (Imp.), and this capacity has also been limited, and the construction of the tank complicated, by grooves and tubes provided to accommodate the passage of control rods.

An auxiliary fuel tank, having a capacity of 6½ gallons (Imp.), is carried inside the hull at a level which would enable it to feed the engine by gravity in an emergency.

Both tanks have their own filler orifices, but the auxiliary tank, which is the more accessible, can be used to fill the main tank through a pipe of 21 mm. inside dia. A cone-type valve is provided in the auxiliary tank to close this passage to the main tank, and presumably this valve is normally closed when both tanks have been filled.

A two-way tap is mounted on the auxiliary tank. In the normal running position, this puts the main tank in direct communication with the engine fuel-pump, but shuts off the feed from the auxiliary tank. In the other position, the connection from the main tank is shut off and the feed to the engine fuel-pump is from the auxiliary tank.

An auxiliary foot-operated diaphragm-type fuel-pump is fitted in the line between the main tank and the two-way valve and is apparently used for priming the engine fuel-pump.

The main tank is provided with a remote level-gauge of the electric type. Both fuel tanks are vented separately by pipes extending well above the fuel level inside the hull.

CHASSIS LUBRICATION

Oil is supplied under pressure by a tapping from the engine main oiling system for the lubrication of the steering knuckles, all ball-and-pin connections in the steering linkage, vertical spindles for the steering bell-cranks and the bearings for the change-speed levers, brake cross-shafts and pedal shafts.

After leaving the engine, the oil passes to a valve which is mounted on the steering column and controlled by a small lever. Apparently this has only two positions, " on " and " off," and by its use the driver can give a feed from the engine for any period desired. After leaving this valve, the oil is piped to a number of distribution or junction boxes provided with metering arrangements of the air-bottle type originally known as " Enots." From these junction boxes, numerous pipes of 4 mm. outside dia. take the oil to the various bearings. The steering knuckles, and other parts having motion relative to the frame, are connected by short lengths of flexible piping. In some cases, the oil is led to one end of a part and distributed to several bearings by drillings in the part, an example of this being the steering drag-links and the steering levers.

ELECTRICAL EQUIPMENT

A complete analysis of the electrical system could not be made owing to the damaged condition of the wiring when the vehicles were received.

The dynamo, starter motor, and magneto were examined by Messrs. C. A. V. Ltd., who reported that these units were similar to units of German tanks for which detailed reports have already been submitted.

The principal particulars of these units appear in the section giving General Data of the complete vehicle (page 8).

It is worth noting that a solenoid is used for controlling the 12-24 volt change-over switch.

HULL

The main hull is divided into two sections, bolted together at a vertical flanged joint approximately in line with the radiator, the rear section being readily detachable for access to the engine.

Both sections are of welded construction, employing surface-hardened armour plate with a Brinell hardness figure of 450-500.

The whole of the interior of the hull is well arranged for stowage and there is ample space for the crew.

The front driver has a fairly wide field of vision, but the length of the engine cover curtails the rear driver's line of sight. Schutzglaser laminated glass blocks, 10½ in. long, 2½ in. wide and 2 in. thick, protect the drivers' vision ports. All other vision slots are backed by thin laminated glass blocks. The transmission of light through a similar glass block removed from a German PZKWIII tank in Libya was found to be 61.5 per cent. as measured by a Craik visual photometer.

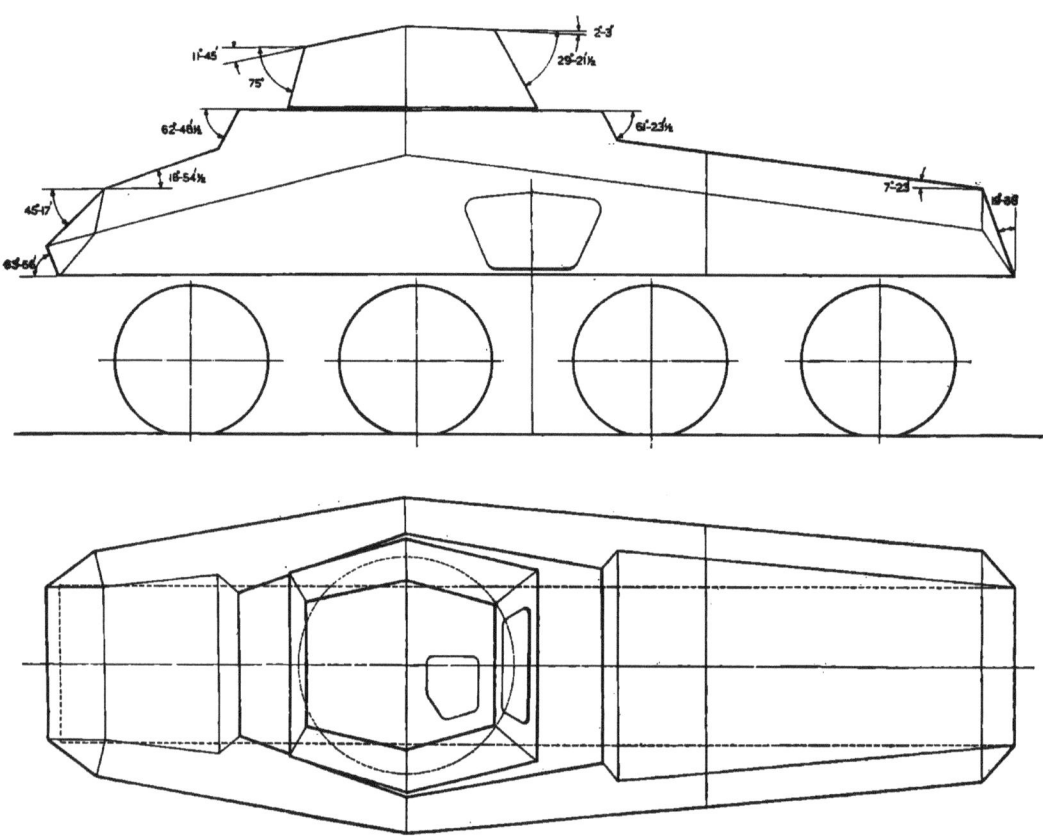

Fig. 54. Elevation and plan of the body and turret, showing the armour-angles.

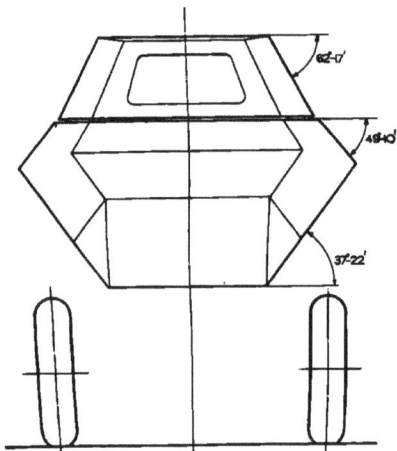

Fig. 55. Rear view of the body and turret, showing the armour-angles.

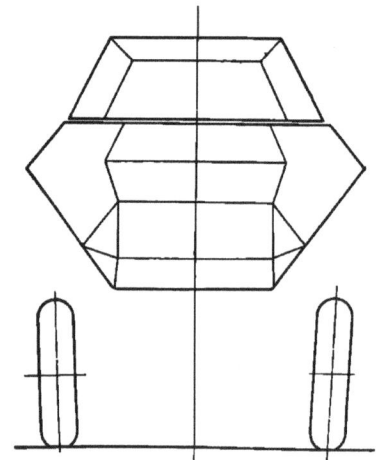

Fig. 56. The planes of intersection of the armour-plating are illustrated in this front view of body and turret.

TURRET

This unit is constructed of single-skin surface-hardened armour plate with a Brinell hardness figure of 450-500. All plates are joined by welding.

The slopes of all plates, and the general contours of the turret, are shown in Figs. 54, 55 and 56.

For the exclusion of dirt from the outside of the ball races, a steel hoop surrounding the balls is recessed into the flange of the gear ring and projects to fit into a corresponding groove in the turret base.

Two independent means of rotating the turret are

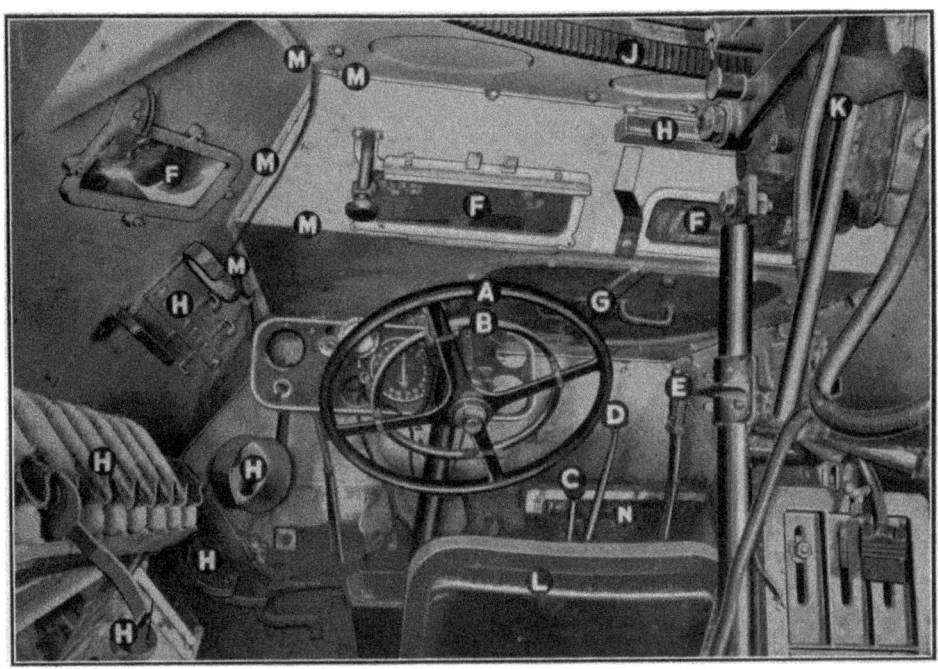

Fig. 57. Inside the hull—the front driver's controls. A. Inverted steering wheel. B. Horn press ring. C. Transfer box lever. D. Gearshift lever. E. Folding hand brake. F. Vision slots. G. Driver's escape hatch. H. Stowage racks and bins. J. Fixed toothed turret ring. K. Gun mounting. L. Driver's seat. M. Welded hull joints. N. Battery.

The seats for the Commander and gunner are mounted on a tubular frame work, suspended from the turret, thus eliminating any need for a rotating floor. The left-hand seat is intended for the Commander.

The Commander has a periscope which may be swung up into position when required.

The turret rotates on a large-diameter ball bearing seated on an internal spur gear ring which is bolted to the top of the hull. Whereas in the case of German tanks hitherto examined, the turret ball bearing is of the radial type, in the Bussing-NAG vehicle, this bearing is of the thrust type, i.e. having one race above and the other below the balls.

In the German tanks referred to, the turret bearing is of the deep-groove type and therefore serves to locate the turret against forces tending to lift it, but, in the case of the machine now under review, it has been necessary to provide eight special C-shaped brackets, the lower arms of which are provided with rollers bearing against the under side of the gear ring.

The turret bearing has 134 balls of 19 mm. dia., and between these, except at one point, are interspaced 133 balls of 13 mm. dia., which serve to prevent the weight-carrying balls from being subject to sliding action against one another.

The thrust race and the teeth of the gear ring are protected by an annular sheet-aluminium guard, made in sections which fit between the brackets provided for holding down the turret.

provided. There is a high-geared quick-acting auxiliary control at the left of the Commander, while the gunner controls a separate combined gear for rotating the turret with a greater degree of accuracy and for elevating the guns.

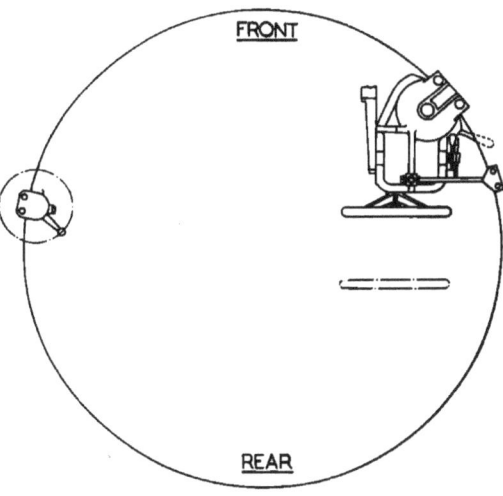

Fig. 58. The relative positions occupied by the Commander's and the Gunner's traversing controls.

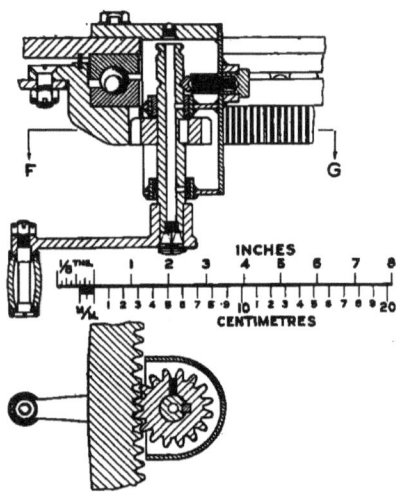

Fig. 59. Vertical and horizontal sections of the Commander's traversing control, with details of the plunger holding the pinion in or out of mesh with the gear ring.

The Commander's control (Fig. 59) consists of a crank handle at the base of a vertical spindle, on the upper end of which is a pinion capable of being meshed with the turret gear ring by axial movement. A spring-loaded plunger holds it in or out of engagement as required.

The combined traversing and elevating control shown in Figs. 60-63 is an assembly mounted in front of, and operated by, the gunner. A split aluminium casing, secured to the top and bottom plates of the turret, houses the majority of the mechanism. Rotation of the hand-wheel rotates the turret through the medium of a worm engaging with a worm-wheel on a vertical spindle and driving, through a friction-disc clutch, a spur pinion constantly in mesh with the turret gear ring. Clockwise motion of the hand wheel turns the turret in the same direction, and vice versa. The clutch appears to fulfil two functions; in the first place it can be disengaged by an external hand lever to provide free movement for the Commander's quick-acting operation, and secondly, it provides a cushioning effect in the event of a severe blow to the turret, as the small lead angle of

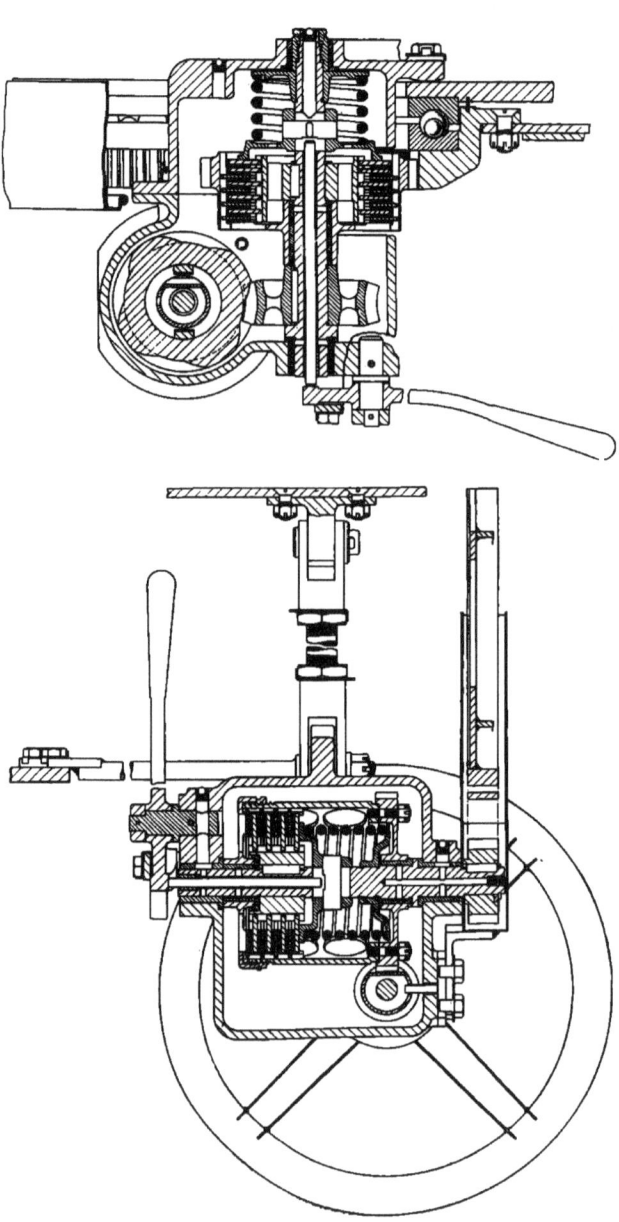

Fig. 60. A vertical section through the clutch and pinion of the Gunner's traversing control, showing also the turret-support ball race.

Fig. 61. A cross-sectional view through the clutch of the elevating control, showing the lever and cam by which it is disengaged.

the worm appears to make the latter irreversible.

Elevation of the guns is obtained by axial movement of the hand-wheel which causes a rack to turn a spur gear. Through a second friction clutch, also manually controlled, this operates a further spur pinion which meshes with a toothed sector connected to the hinged gun-mounting. A sheet-steel guard covers the sector teeth. The range of elevation obtainable is approximately one-third of that provided by the gun-mounting, and it appears that the clutch is provided to enable a fresh relative setting of hand-wheel to elevation to be obtained.

Constructionally, the hand-wheel shaft is arranged co-axially with a steel tube incorporating a rack, and prevented from relative end-wise movement by a shoulder at the wheel end and by a collar keyed and nutted to the shaft at the other end. Longitudinal slots in the outer circumference of the collar engage with two long keys plug-welded in the bore of the worm, so that the latter receives rotary, but not axial, movement.

A longitudinal slot in the racked tube engages with a guide bolted in the casing, which prevents rotation.

An interesting detail in the design of the rack is that the latter is a flat steel strip of suitable thickness for the teeth, arc welded into the tube, with end-pieces also welded in position, and the whole subsequently machined.

The two friction clutches mentioned above are of conventional multiple-disc type.

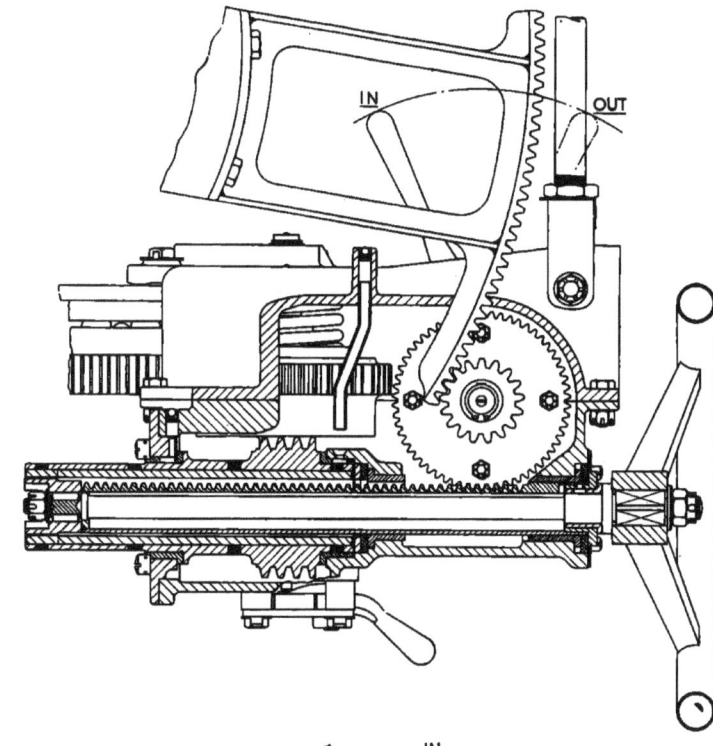

Fig. 62. A longitudinal section of the Gunner's control that shows the rack and other details of the elevating gear.

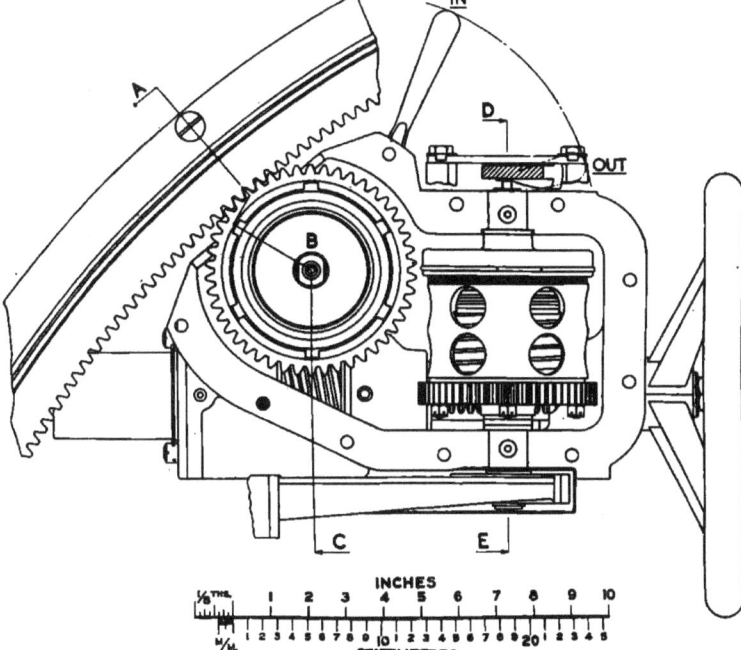

Fig. 63. The upper casing of the Gunner's control has been removed, displaying the clutch-drums.

DATA OF TURRET-CONTROL CLUTCHES

Particulars	Turret Rotation	Gun Elevation
No. of friction discs	9	7
Outside dia. of friction discs	109 mm.	92 mm.
Inside dia. of friction discs	80 mm.	62 mm.
Thickness of friction discs	2 mm.	2 mm.
Rate per inch of coil spring	224 lb.	50 lb.
Spring pressure (clutch in)	168 lb.	100 lb.
Torque to slip clutch (assuming .27 coefficient of friction)	760 lb. in.	284 lb. in.
Effort at handwheel rim to slip clutch	22.4 lb.	12.4 lb.

Table 24

The friction discs float between the driving and driven steel plates, and appear to be of the normal asbestos-composition material.

The engagement and disengagement of each clutch is controlled by axial movement of a rod loosely fitted in the hollow clutch shaft, this endwise movement being effected by the face-cam formed on the clutch-operating lever. The slope of this cam is such that the control lever is self-locking in any position of the range available. No adjustment is provided for the clutch spring tension; such provision would appear to be unnecessary considering the large initial deflection of the clutch spring in relation to any wear which might take place.

To enable the clutches to work dry, the main casing does not function as an oil bath; for lubrication of the bearings and the worm gears, individual oil-cup fittings of the ball-valve type, suitable for oil-can lubrication, are provided.

DATA OF TURRET GEARS

Part	Module	Tooth Width (mm.)	Brinell Hardness	No. of Teeth	Ratio : 1	Gear Centres (mm.)
AUXILIARY TRAVERSING CONTROL						
Pinion on hand wheel	3	18	112	16	27.25	630
Gear Ring		26	—	436		
PRINCIPAL TRAVERSING CONTROL						
Primary Gearing { Worm (right hand)		40	111	4	5.75 ⎫ Overall ratio 54.5	83.8
Primary Gearing { Worm-wheel		30	101	23		
Secondary Gearing { Spur pinion	3	20	106	46	9.48 ⎭	585
Secondary Gearing { Gear Ring		26	—	436		
GUN ELEVATION CONTROL						
Primary Gearing { Rack (max. travel 200 mm.)	2	15	103	47		
Primary Gearing { Spur Gear		15	109	58		
Secondary Gearing { Spur pinion	3	20	114	17	17.1	460.5
Secondary Gearing { Spur sector		20	87	30		

Max. travel of rack = 11° 35′ elevation of gun.   Max. arc of elevation = 33°.

Table 25

PERFORMANCE

During the trials, this vehicle gave a notably good performance in negotiating steep gradients, crossing wide trenches, and maintaining relatively high speed over rough terrain. In most other respects, the results of the trials, which are recorded in Appendix A, were considered satisfactory. The cooling system was, however, found to be inadequate for tropical conditions.

During prolonged high-speed running, temperature differences of about 140° F. (jacket-water outlet to ambient air) were recorded. These high T.D. figures may be partly attributable to the relatively small frontal area of the radiator.

Signs of erratic action, giving rise to a certain amount of difficulty in control, were noticed in the steering. Certain features of the steering layout of

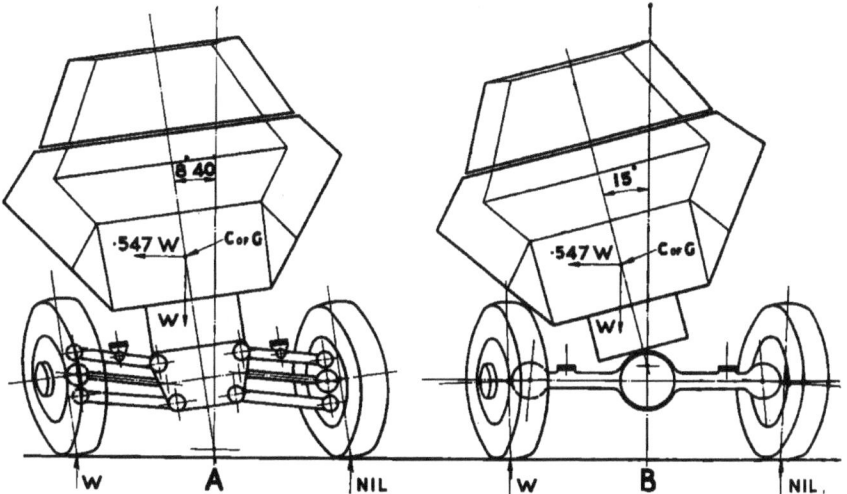

Fig. 64. A diagram to illustrate the effects of full-lock cornering at limit speed.
A. Independent Suspension. B. Rigid Axle.

this vehicle tend, in combination with the suspension, to give rise to instability in the steering control. This instability occurs when the vehicle is turning, and Fig. 64 illustrates the conditions which apply when the speed and radius of the turn are such that the outer tyres are taking all the weight and the inner wheels are about to leave the ground.

View A shows what happens to the German A.F.V. which is the subject of this report, and, by contrast, View B shows what would happen if rigid axles were substituted for independent suspension without changing the steering layout or deflection characteristics of the suspension.

The following specific conditions have therefore been assumed as applying to both cases A and B:—

Total weight of vehicle	17,640 lb.
Weight on 4 outer tyres	17,640 lb.
Weight on 4 inner tyres	0 lb.
Spring centres	37.5 in.
Wheel deflection (free to normal load)	4.75 in.
Height of centre of gravity above ground	46.5 in.
Speed in m.p.h.	11.5
Steering condition	Full Lock

Resultant loads and angles of roll, arising from the above conditions, are considerably different in the two cases under review, as shown in Table 26.

The table and the diagrams illustrate the advantage which independent suspension confers in enabling soft suspension to be adopted without introducing excessive roll when cornering.

On the other hand, it must be pointed out that it would be unusual to adopt such soft springs in a vehicle having rigid axle suspension, and, if the spring-deflection were reduced to the more normal value of about $2\frac{3}{4}$ in., the roll-angle with the rigid-axle suspension would be no greater than with the independent suspension.

Fig. 64 also shows how, in the case of the German A.F.V., the action of the suspension affects the inclination of the steering-knuckle axis, and, under the conditions reviewed, causes this axis to tilt outwardly at the top. This reversal of the normal inclination introduces an unstable condition in the steering, because, in conjunction with the offset between the tyre-contact centre and the steering-knuckle axis, it causes the vehicle to be lifted when straightening out of a turn.

This undesirable condition does not arise in case B, because turning does not affect the inclination of the steering-knuckle axis except to the small extent that is permitted by tyre deflection; as this axis remains tilted outwardly at the bottom, the act of putting on lock automatically lifts the vehicle, and the steering is thus rendered self-centering by gravity.

The above remarks imply no criticism of the type of independent suspension used in this vehicle, it being evident that the designers of the German A.F.V. could have obtained reasonable steering stability either by increasing the outward rake of the steering-knuckle axis or by reducing the offset between this axis and the point of tyre-contact.

Trench Crossing.

A four-wheeled vehicle is incapable of crossing a deep trench having a width greater than the diameter of the vehicle's front tyres. When the front axle reaches the trench, it drops to an extent limited only by the chassis coming into contact with the ground.

Angles of Roll		
	A	B
Centrifugal force at C of G	9,649 lb.	9,649 lb.
Overturning moment	9,649 × 3.84 lb./ft.	9,649 × 3.79 lb./ft.
Righting moment	17,640 × 2.08 lb./ft.	17,640 × 2.05 lb./ft.
Angle of body	8° 40'	15° 0'
Angle per 1,000 lb. force	0° 54'	1° 30'

Table 26

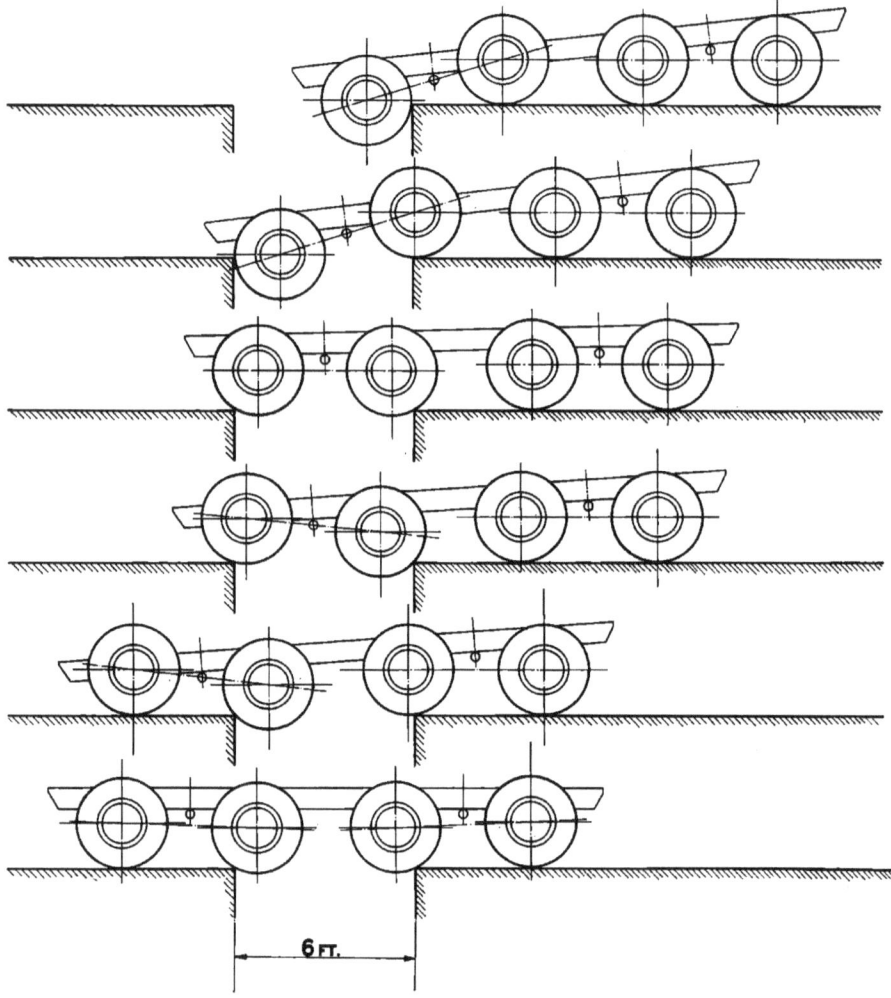

Fig. 65. Illustrating progressive wheel positions when crossing a trench. Note that the depth of trench is immaterial.

When this happens, it is practically impossible for four-wheel drive to extricate the vehicle, even if the transmission does not suffer serious damage.

An eight-wheeled vehicle, however, can readily cross trenches of unlimited depth, provided (1) that their width does not materially exceed the bogie wheelbase of the vehicle, and (2) that the articulation stops have been designed to limit the rise and fall of the wheels to reasonable values.

It was demonstrated that the German A.F.V. could cross a trench over 4 ft. wide, i.e. a few inches less than the vehicle's bogie wheelbase.

Fig. 65 shows what happens when this particular vehicle is crossing trenches, and gives rise to the following conclusions :—

(1) The front wheels cannot climb out of a trench wider than the wheel-diameter if the rise and fall permitted to the axles is excessive.

(2) If the level of the ground on the far side of the trench is higher than that on the near side, the ability to cross is reduced.

(3) If these levels are the same, and articulation is held to reasonable limits by suitable stops, trenches of any depth, and having a width somewhat greater than the bogie wheelbase, can be crossed. It seems probable that the German A.F.V. could cross a trench well over 5 ft. wide.

APPENDIX "A"

ANALYSIS OF PERFORMANCE

WEIGHTS.

	Tons	Cwts.	Qrs.
1st Axle	1	18	3
2nd Axle	1	19	1
3rd Axle	2	0	2
4th Axle	1	19	0
Total	7	17	2

TYRE DEFLECTIONS.

18%—33 lb./sq. in. (giving an effective radius of 16.545″).

BRAKING.

1. Dry level concrete road—Hand = 11.70 f.s.s.
2. Dry level concrete road—Foot = 18.90 f.s.s.
3. Controlled descent of 515 yd. (gradient 1 : 10) :
   Speed   8 m.p.h.
   Gears   Neutral
   Condition of drums   Just Warm
4. Dry concrete gradient of 1 in 2.25, vehicle facing uphill : Held on hand and foot brakes separately.
5. Dry concrete gradient of 1 in 2.25, vehicle facing downhill : Held on hand and foot brakes separately.

ACCELERATION.

Standing ¼ mile (mean of two runs, one in either direction) = 26.4 m.p.h.

SPEED.

1. Flying ¼ mile (mean of two runs, one in either direction) = 49.05 m.p.h.
2. Ascent of 515 yd. of road, average gradient 1 in 10. Flying start = 21.55 m.p.h.
3. Ascent of 515 yd. of road, average gradient 1 in 10. Standing start = 16.3 m.p.h.

HILL-CLIMBING.

1. Dry concrete gradient of 1 in 2.25 : Stopped and restarted successfully. No wheel spin.
2. Loose gravel gradient of 1 in 2.43. Stopped and restarted successfully. Slight wheel spin.

ROAD TRIAL. (Road dry, little traffic.)

Average speed over 50 miles = 33.1 m.p.h.

CROSS-COUNTRY TRIALS.

1. 2-mile circuit, dry and dusty :
   Standing start, forward = 19.7 m.p.h.
2. 2-mile circuit, dry and dusty :
   Standing start, in reverse = 19.0 m.p.h.
3. 40 miles, dry and dusty = 16.43 m.p.h.

FUEL CONSUMPTION.

1. Road   5.43 m.p.g. (range 165 miles)
2. Cross-country 3.80 m.p.g. (range 110 miles)

ANGLE OF OVER-TURN.

30° measured on hull.

TILTING.

11½° slope, engine running and front of vehicle across slope in both directions and pointing up and down. No leakage of fuel, oil or water in any direction.

TURNING CIRCLES.

Right- and left-hand locks = 37 ft. 5 in.

TRENCH CROSSING

Crossed 4 ft. 1 in. revetted trench with no spoil successfully.

CENTRE OF BALANCE.

Measured from Centre-Line of front wheels = 6 ft. 9 in.

BELLY CLEARANCE.

12 in. to front differential housing.

WADING.

2 ft. 0 in. limited by starter solenoid box.

SALVAGE.

Hooks are adequate for towing or being towed cross-country.

DISTORTION.

No interferences or mechanical derangement with frame fully distorted.

APPENDIX "B"

ANALYSIS OF COMPONENTS

Part	CHEMICAL ANALYSIS (PERCENTAGES)																Brinell No.	General Description of Material
	C Total	C Combined	Si	Mn	S	P	Ni	Cr	Mo	W	Al	Cu	Fe	Mg	Zn			
Piston			14.05				1.30				Base	.30	Trace	2.03	Nil			Aluminium Alloy Casting
Valve		.30	.94				13.26	16.7		2.85			Base			241		Nickel-Chrome-Tungsten
Con. Rod.		.44		.68	.019	.014	Nil	Nil					Base			201		Steel Stamping
Gudgeon Pin		.16	.25	.55			.13	.64	Trace				Base			640–668		Case-hardened Chrome Steel Bar (Case .030" deep)
Big-end Stud		.30		.65			3.41	.75	Nil				Base			241		Nickel-Chrome Steel Bar
Cylinder Liner	2.94	.54	2.43	.87	.087	.164	Nil	Nil					Base			to 478		C.I. Casting
Tappet	3.26	.56	2.57	.78	.094	.134	Nil	Nil					Base	Head chilled Stem chilled		–444 to 285		Chilled C.I.
Tappet Guide	3.34	.56	2.22	.79	.109	.160	Nil	Nil					Base			229		C.I.
Clutch Plate	3.47		2.50	.59	.083	.246	.54	Nil					Base			201		Nickel-Iron Casting
Starter Ring		.55		.65			Nil	Nil					Base			201		Carbon Steel
Crankshaft		.40		.74			.39	1.21					Base			*		Flame-hardened Carbon Steel
Balance Weight		.38		.53			Nil	Nil					Base					Carbon Steel
Stub Axle		.30		.99			Nil	Nil					Base					Carbon-Manganese Stamping
Suspension Link		.41		.72			.10	.96					Base					Stamping
Diff. Housing		.45		.44			Nil	Nil					Base					Steel Casting
Diff. Plunger		1.00					.26	1.50					Base			648		Ball-bearing Steel

* Hardness of Journals and Pins varies from Brinell 494 to 590. Brinell hardness of Webs, 339

www.ingramcontent.com/pod-product-compliance
Lightning Source LLC
Chambersburg PA
CBHW061056170426
43193CB00025B/2992